D0164146

dieppe 1942

prelude to d-day

KEN FORD

dieppe 1942

prelude to d-day

Praeger Illustrated Military History Series

Westport, Connecticut
London

Library of Congress Cataloging-in-Publication Data

Ford, Ken, 1943–
    Dieppe 1942 : prelude to D-Day / Ken Ford.
      p. cm – (Praeger illustrated military history, ISSN 1547-206X)
    Originally published: Oxford: Osprey, 2003.
    Includes bibliographical references and index.
    ISBN 0-275-98281-5 (alk. paper)
    1. Dieppe Raid, 1942. I. Title. II. Series.
    D756.5.D5F67   2004
    940.54'21425–dc22 2003063263

British Library Cataloguing in Publication Data is available.

First published in paperback in 2003 by Osprey Publishing Limited, Elms Court,
Chapel Way, Botley, Oxford OX2 9LP. All rights reserved.

Copyright © 2004 by Osprey Publishing Limited

Library of Congress Catalog Card Number: 2003063263
ISBN: 0-275-98281-5
ISSN: 1547-206X

Praeger Publishers, 88 Post Road West, Westport, CT 06881
An imprint of Greenwood Publishing Group, Inc.
www.praeger.com

Printed in China through World Print Ltd.

The paper used in this book complies with the Permanent Paper Standard issued
by the National Information Standards Organization (Z39.48-1984).

10   9   8   7   6   5   4   3   2   1

FRONT COVER: HU1904, courtesy of the Imperial War Museum, London

ILLUSTRATED BY: Howard Gerrard

CONTENTS

KEY TO MILITARY SYMBOLS

XXXXX	XXXX	XXX	XX	X
ARMY GROUP	ARMY	CORPS	DIVISION	BRIGADE
III	II	I		
REGIMENT	BATTALION	COMPANY	INFANTRY	CAVALRY
ARTILLERY	ARMOUR	MECHANISED	AIRBORNE	SPECIAL FORCES

ORIGINS OF THE BATTLE

After the British Expeditionary Force was ejected from France at Dunkirk in 1940, Britain conducted a vigorous programme of raids against German-held territory. From Norway to St Nazaire, Commandos took the fight back to the occupied coastline of Hitler's Europe, harassing his garrisons and tying down his forces. Although these incursions were no more than pinpricks on the thick hide of the Nazi Empire, they did boost morale at home and engender an offensive spirit within the armed forces.

In the summer of 1942, after almost three years of war, the Allied position was grim. Across the globe the tide of war was flowing against Britain and her Commonwealth. Japan's rampant progress in the Far East was menacing India, in North Africa the British army was in headlong retreat, the German army was driving on Stalingrad and the River Volga, threatening to overwhelm the Russians, and German U-boats were ravaging the nation's supply lines, sinking more than 1,500,000 tons of shipping during May and June. Whilst it was true there was a glimmer of hope after the United States entered the war, good news was sparse.

RIGHT **Canadian survivors of Operation Jubilee arrive back in Newhaven after the raid on Dieppe. Their faces show the relief of having made it back to safety; their wounds and dishevelled appearance recall their hellish experiences. (National Archives of Canada, PA-183775)**

OPPOSITE **Lieutenant Wallace of the Calgary Tanks moving amongst the dead on Dieppe's town beach. (Bundesarchiv 101/291/1205/35A)**

America could do little until her forces were fully mobilised. The USA and Russia, as well as public opinion at home, urged Britain to open a 'second front' against Europe to help relieve pressure on the Eastern Front and assist Russia in her efforts to stem German expansion. Britain did not have the means available, however, to launch a full-scale invasion of Europe. She was already heavily committed in the Far East, Middle East and North Africa. At home those divisions that were fully trained lacked the equipment and expertise to mount a sustained campaign across the Channel. Amphibious warfare at that time was still not an exact art and much development and application was required before the army, navy and air force could act as an integrated force.

Although Britain was not ready to launch an invasion, the nation could at least hit back at the enemy through its programme of attacks against occupied France. Such acts helped to tie down German troops and force Hitler to commit men and materiel to the protection of the northern coastline of his growing empire, resources that could have been used against the Russians. But even with a large number of units static in France and the Low Countries, the Russians still had to contend with the vast bulk of Hitler's forces. Only 46 German divisions were based in Europe, whilst Hitler had over 200 divisions in the east engaged with the Red Army.

British raids against mainland Europe were planned and executed by a branch of the services called Combined Operations. The organisation was not a service in its own right, but had to rely on the co-operation of the Royal Navy and Royal Air Force to provide the means to carry out

Landing Craft Personnel Large – LCP(L) – which were used in the raid, after their return to Newhaven. This type of landing craft carried 22 fully laden troops across the Channel and onto the beaches. The craft shown here are from the Sixth Flotilla, Group Six, which took the Queen's Own Cameron Highlanders into Green Beach at Pourville. (Imperial War Museum, H22606)

its forays against the enemy. It did, however, have its own troops of army commandos, but their light weapons and special skills precluded large-scale attacks. They were more suitable for 'hit and run' raids. In March 1942 the head of Combined Operations, Lord Louis Mountbatten, joined the Chiefs of Staff Committee, which then nominally put Combined Operations on equal terms with the army, navy and air force.

The pressure, both of public opinion and from Britain's allies, for more affirmative action against the enemy and to aid Russia was keenly felt by Churchill. He proposed raids or lodgements in Norway and the Cherbourg Peninsula, both of which were rejected as being unsuitable. Instead, his Chiefs of Staff suggested a large-scale raid against a port close to the Pas de Calais coastline, within the protective range of the aircraft of Fighter Command. Seven such ports were examined and then rejected for various reasons before it was decided to look elsewhere. The next closest port along the coast was Dieppe. It was located just 70 miles across the Channel from Newhaven, close enough to allow the approach for a surprise dawn attack to be made under the cover of darkness. It was also well within the RAF's fighter umbrella and had a useful harbour. Of all the sites proposed for a major landing, Dieppe offered the best prospects. On 4 April 1942 Mountbatten gave orders to his staff at Combined Operations to draw up plans for an attack.

Two separate plans were presented by Mountbatten's staff to the Chiefs of Staff Committee for consideration. The first plan proposed landing tanks and infantry on either side of Dieppe and capturing the town in a pincer movement over the two headlands that flank the port. The second plan was for a frontal assault across the town's beach, with support from landings on the flanks to the east and west. The two heavy gun batteries that commanded the approaches to Dieppe were located at Varengeville and Berneval and they would be seized and destroyed by airborne troops in advance of the landings. Both plans proposed a 'reconnaissance in force' rather than a simple raid, seeking to gain experience of large-scale amphibious landings and to test the support

services' ability to land and maintain assault forces ashore. On 18 April 1942 the Committee decided that planning should go ahead for the raid based on the second plan. The Chiefs of Staff agreed that the main weight of the landings should be made by a frontal assault over the town's beach, preceded by a heavy bombing attack.

The operation for the raid on Dieppe was given the codename 'Rutter' and was planned to take place during a period of suitable tides in early July. The proposed size of the venture made it larger than anything previously undertaken by Combined Operations. It was too large and complicated for army Commandos to carry out alone – regular troops from Home Forces would have to be involved. Lieutenant-General Bernard Montgomery's South Eastern Command, located in the area from which the attack would be launched, would provide the necessary troops. He decided that the Canadian troops already in South Eastern Command would make the assault, although Montgomery later claimed that the decision to use them was not his, but came from his superior, General Sir Bernard Paget.

By 1942 there was considerable pressure from many quarters for some sort of Canadian involvement in offensive action against the enemy. The first Canadian troops had landed in England in December 1939 and by the summer of 1942 over 200,000 of them had arrived. They had spent almost three years training and performing guard duties along the Channel coast. By then, three infantry and two armoured divisions had been raised, along with several armoured brigades and heavy artillery formations. These years of boredom and relative inactivity led to morale problems. The Canadian Army was an all-volunteer force and the men were keen to get at the enemy. It was no surprise then that when the commander of Canadian forces in Britain, Lieutenant-General R.G.L. McNaughton, was asked to provide the troops required for the Dieppe raid he jumped at the chance for his men to see action. He proposed that the Canadian 2nd Division be used in the operation.

The size of the intended raid was larger than anything yet mounted, with all three of the services contributing large numbers to the operation. Over 6,000 troops were to land and the Royal Navy was tasked with transporting them across the Channel, putting them safely ashore and then evacuating them back to England once the operation was over. Warships would also provide supporting fire against enemy installations during the attack. The RAF would protect the assault forces from interference by enemy aircraft by putting in the air the most powerful fighter cover seen since the Battle of Britain.

On 9 May the main components of the operation had been identified by Mountbatten's staff and the official outline plan was put before the Chiefs of Staff Committee and adopted. Intelligence reports suggested that Dieppe was not heavily defended and that the beaches in the vicinity were suitable for landing infantry and armoured vehicles. Although there were some misgivings, most notably from Mountbatten, about the main attack being made by frontal assault on the most heavily defended sector of Dieppe's town beach, most were optimistic about the outcome of the raid.

With approval received, Operation Rutter was planned to take place between 4 and 8 July. After weeks of training the troops were assembled and embarked on their craft during the first few days of July, but the order to sail was never given. The critical period of tides suitable for the attack came during a bout of very unsettled weather. On 7 July enemy planes spotted the convoys of ships in the Solent and bombed them. Little damage was done but it now seemed that the enemy might be alerted to the possibility of some sort of amphibious operation. Coupled with an even greater deterioration in the weather, this resulted in the operation being abandoned. The troops disembarked and were dispersed back to South Eastern Command.

Everyone imagined that this would be the end of the raid, but Mountbatten and his team thought otherwise. They had already seen many other previous operations cancelled and they were confident that the Dieppe plan was good enough to warrant another try. Mountbatten lobbied Churchill and the Chiefs of Staff and eventually the attack was reinstated, despite grave doubts about certain aspects of security. It was common knowledge, even to those not participating in the operation, that the objective of Operation Rutter had been Dieppe. Too many people were now party to its objectives and the desire to see the attack carried out was beginning to overwhelm prudent caution. Nonetheless, approval had been given from the very top so the raid was definitely back on. Mountbatten's staff now resumed planning of the 'reconnaissance in force' on Dieppe. A new outline plan was formed with a new codename, 'Jubilee', and was scheduled to take place during the middle of August.

CHRONOLOGY

Canadian troops of 2nd Infantry Division on exercise in the Isle of Wight before the raid. The men are practising evacuating casualties onto infantry assault landing craft (LCA). (National Archives of Canada, C-017293)

1942

4 April Admiral Mountbatten, Commander Combined Operations, asks his staff to draw up proposals for a large raid against Dieppe. The objects of the operation are to carry out a reconnaissance in depth and to challenge German occupation troops in an attempt to relieve pressure on the Eastern Front.

18 April Chiefs of Staff Committee agrees to a 'reconnaissance in force' against Dieppe, codenamed 'Rutter', to take place in early July.

30 April Canadian 2nd Infantry Division is chosen to carry out the attack.

May–June Canadian troops move to the Isle of Wight and undergo intensive training for the operation.

2 July In the face of worsening weather, troops are embarked on board the assault convoys in the Solent ready to carry out Operation Rutter.

7 July The convoy of ships carrying the forces destined for Dieppe is bombed at anchor in the Solent by German aircraft. The operation is abandoned due to continuing bad weather and the assault forces are disbanded.

22 July The Dieppe operation is reinstated. Combined Operations make some changes to the plan, including substituting Commandos for airborne forces to capture the large German coastal batteries. The operation is given the new codename 'Jubilee'.

18 August Embarkation of the forces taking part in Jubilee begins in five ports along the south coast. The force has been dispersed for security and safety reasons. During the evening the attack force sails for Dieppe from Southampton, Portsmouth, Gosport, Shoreham and Newhaven.

19 August

0155hrs The seaborne force passes safely through the German minefields in mid-Channel.

0320hrs All troop-carrying ships have reached their lowering positions and all have loaded and launched their assault landing craft. The groups who have crossed the Channel in Eureka boats line up for the run in to the beaches.

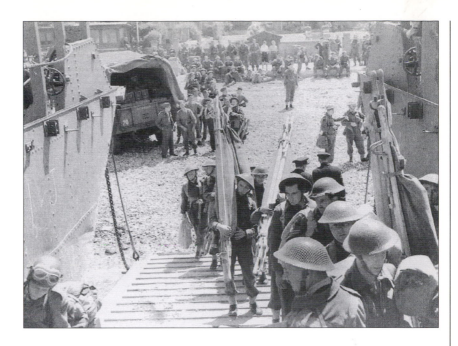

Canadian troops practise loading a landing craft tank (LCT) for casualty evacuation. This peaceful setting on the Isle of Wight is complete with local children in the background watching the action. (National Archives of Canada, PA-113244)

0343hrs Flotilla of landing craft carrying 3 Commando and heading for Yellow Beach run into a German convoy off Dieppe. In the ensuing sea battle the group is dispersed and several craft are damaged.

0445hrs Lieutenant Buckee brings LCP 15 into Yellow II Beach with its lone party of 3 Commando lead by Capt Peter Young. Six other surviving craft from 3 Commando land on Yellow I Beach 30 minutes later (**0515hrs**). Neither of these groups is strong enough to attack 'Goebbels' Battery. Young's party interfere with the operation of the German guns, but is later forced to withdraw. All of the Commandos on Yellow I Beach are either killed or captured.

0450hrs 4 Commando lands on Orange I and II Beaches to begin its attack on 'Hess' Battery at Varengeville.

0450hrs The South Saskatchewans land on Green Beach and take the village of Pourville, but are prevented from advancing eastwards to Dieppe by fierce enemy fire.

0506hrs The Royal Regiment of Canada land on Blue Beach 16 minutes late. The delay means that it is lighter than had been anticipated and the enemy are roused and ready. Heavy fire

Men of Canadian 2nd Division disembarking from LCTs during training on the Isle of Wight. It was planned to use LCTs to take men off the beaches out to the landing ships offshore once the raid was over. (National Archives of Canada, PA-113243)

decimates the battalion. Further waves of infantry are landed but, with the exception of a few individuals, the whole battalion is trapped on the beach and virtually wiped out. Just a handful of men escape death or capture.

0523hrs After a preliminary bombardment by warships and a bombing raid, the Essex Scottish and the Royal Hamilton Light Infantry land over Red and White Beaches in front of Dieppe town. The armour of the Calgary Tanks is late arriving and the two infantry battalions are met with a hail of enemy fire that pins them to the beach.

0533hrs The first Churchill tanks arrive at Dieppe. All are landed, but the LCTs bringing them in are either lost or damaged. Some tanks get off the beach onto the promenade, while others flounder in the loose shingle. Within 30 minutes two further waves arrive, only to be immobilised on the water's edge or disabled by enemy fire. None of the tanks are able to push inland from the seafront into the town. Concrete barricades bar all exits.

0543hrs A lucky shot from the 2in. mortars of 4 Commando hits some ammunition within 'Hess' Battery and the whole gun position is wiped out by a gigantic explosion and fireball and remains out of action.

0550hrs The Cameron Highlanders land on Green Beach at Pourville into fierce enemy fire. Their CO is the first man killed. The battalion is split either side of the River Scie, unable to consolidate. Those troops on the east bank of the River Scie join with the South Saskatchewans to clear the eastern hill, whilst the remainder under Major Low move down the river valley in an effort to link up with the tanks landing at Dieppe and attack the airfield at St Aubin.

0615hrs The arrival of armour over Red and White Beaches allows some of the infantry to get off the beach. A few men from the Essex Scottish make it across the promenade and into the houses, but are quickly killed, captured or forced back to the beach. On the right the Hamiltons take the Casino building and push a few men into the town, but these too are soon forced back.

0630hrs Immediately after 'Hess' Battery has been strafed by Spitfire aircraft, Lord Lovat's 4 Commando storms the gun positions and eliminate its garrison. The guns are destroyed and 4 Commando begins its orderly withdrawal to Orange II Beach and home.

0704hrs The Military Force Commander, MajGen Roberts, decides the time has come to reinforce the landings at Dieppe for a concerted push onto the western heights and sends in his floating reserve, Les Fusiliers Mont-Royal. The battalion is landed on the hostile beach only to be thrown into confusion by the enemy fire. The fresh troops can do no more than seek shelter from the carnage.

The beach at Dieppe in 1944. In the left foreground are the ruins of the Casino, demolished by the Germans after the raid. (Ken Ball/Canada Dept. Of National Defence/National Archives of Canada, PA-183100)

Blue Beach at Puys. On the left is the high sea wall that caused so much trouble to the Royal Regiment of Canada. In the distance, less than a mile away, is the harbour entrance of Dieppe. (Ken Ford)

Motor Launch ML 270 shepherds four LCPs as they group together prior to the run in to the beaches. The troops are from Les Fusiliers Mont-Royal, the Canadian 2nd Division's floating reserve. (National Archives of Canada, PA-113247)

0830hrs Roberts believes that things have stabilised on the beach at Dieppe and now decides to send in the Royal Marine A Commando to attack the eastern headland. Appalled by the chaos and death on the beach the marines' CO, LtCol Picton-Phillips, signals for his men to abandon the landings. He is mortally wounded and only six craft turn away, the other two continue, carrying their men to death or captivity.

0845hrs The advance of Major Law's Camerons inland from Green Beach brings them to a point above Petit Appeville. They discover, however, that the enemy already hold the bridge over the River Scie in strength. There is no sign of the tanks from Dieppe.

0900hrs Major-General Roberts accepts that the attack is failing and that the objectives of the raid will not be achieved. Preparations are made to withdraw the troops from the beaches.

0930hrs The Camerons abandon their advance on St Aubin, having penetrated further than any other Allied troops.

1045hrs Landing craft start to arrive to begin the hazardous task of taking men off the beaches. In extreme acts of heroism, the naval crews manage to save many, but many more are lost in the attempt. The only choices left to those troops that cannot make it to the few rescue boats are surrender or death.

1240hrs The Naval and Military Force Commanders aboard HMS *Calpe* come close inshore to make a final inspection of Red and White Beaches. Under enemy fire they steam past Dieppe. No troops can be seen alive on the beaches. The dead litter the shoreline and those men who have survived are marching away into captivity. HMS *Calpe* turns for home – Operation Jubilee is over.

The Canadian 14th Tank Battalion (Calgary Tanks) was equipped with the Churchill heavy infantry tank. This example has lost a track on the beach immobilising it. The loose shingle on the beach created traction problems for the tanks. Pebbles and stones were sometimes forced up between the tracks and the drive wheels, tearing the track off. (Bundesarchiv, 101/362/2208/10A)

OPPOSING COMMANDERS

ALLIED COMMANDERS

Between the cancellation of Operation Rutter and the reinstatement of the attack on Dieppe under the title of Jubilee, Gen Montgomery left South Eastern Command to assume command of British 8th Army in North Africa, but not before he voiced his disapproval of the operation being launched against the same objective. In a letter to his superior, General Paget, Montgomery urged that another target be chosen because of the likelihood that security had been compromised. It was too late – everyone concerned was caught up in a wave of optimism, convinced not only that the operation's objectives were achievable but that security and surprise had not been compromised.

In view of the large numbers of Canadian troops involved in the raid, it was decided that a senior Canadian officer would now exercise overall charge of the operation. Lieutenant-General Harry Crerar, Commander Canadian I Corps, took over Montgomery's responsibilities and guided the project through to execution. Crerar reported directly to Gen McNaughton who commanded all Canadian forces in Britain.

Lieutenant-General R.G.L. McNaughton was a career soldier then aged 55 years. He had served in France as an artillery officer in the First World War, where he was twice wounded in action and won the DSO. Between the wars, he remained in the army and held a succession of staff and field posts. McNaughton arrived in England with the first contingent of Canadian soldiers in December 1939, soon after Britain declared war on Germany.

Lieutenant-General Robert McNaughton studies a map with the British Prime Minister, Winston Churchill. MacNaughton was head of all Canadian forces in England and had arrived with the first contingent from Canada in November 1939. (National Archives of Canada, PA-119399)

Vice Admiral Lord Louis Mountbatten, Commander Combined Operations, visits Canadian troops prior to Operation Jubilee. Mountbatten was the driving force behind the Dieppe raid, although he did not agree with the final alterations made to the plans. (Imperial War Museum, A13219)

Over the next few years this force grew in size to become Canadian I Corps and then, finally, in 1944 Canadian First Army.

Lieutenant-General Harry Crerar had also served in the Great War, rising from subaltern to lieutenant-colonel, seeing action with the Canadian Expeditionary Force on the Western Front. In 1940 Crerar came to England as head of the Canadian planning staff. Later that year he returned to Canada as Chief of General Staff in Canada, before returning once again to Britain to command Canadian I Corps. He was 54 years old at the time of Dieppe.

Operation Jubilee had inherited the basic objectives of Rutter. A brigade from Canadian 2nd Infantry Division would make the frontal assault on Dieppe, whilst battalions from another of the division's brigades attacked on either flank. There was, however, a fundamental change made to the method of eliminating the heavy coastal batteries to the extreme east and west of the town. Airborne troops would no longer be used. Commandos from 3 and 4 Commando, landing from the sea, would assault the two German batteries.

Major-General John Hamilton Roberts commanded Canadian 2nd Infantry Division. He had taken over the division during the winter of 1941–42 when the existing commander was deemed too old for a field command and sent back to Canada. Roberts was 50 years old and had served with the Royal Canadian Horse Artillery in France during the First War, where he had been wounded and had won the Military Cross. His arrival in the division saw the exit of many elderly, long-serving officers and their replacement by younger men. Roberts then instigated a vigorous programme of exercises and manoeuvres in an effort to bring the division up to a state of battle readiness.

The two British Commandos that were to land with the Canadians were led by young men with battle experience. **Lieutenant-Colonel John Durnford-Slater** commanded 3 Commando, whilst **Lieutenant-Colonel The Lord Lovat** commanded 4 Commando. Durnford-Slater claimed to have been the first commando when units were raised in 1940, with Lord Lovat also being a very early volunteer. Both had already participated in raids against the enemy, Durnford-Slater had led 3 Commando against Vaagsö while Lord Lovat had taken part in the Lofoten raid in 1941 with 4 Commando.

The Naval Force Commander, **Captain John Hughes-Hallet**, was Naval Advisor to Combined Operations and had been involved in the planning of the enterprise from the beginning, being the first to propose Dieppe as a likely target. Hughes-Hallet had been the naval planner for the commando attack on the dry docks at St Nazaire in March 1942 and had already been involved in the preparation of many other combined operations.

Air cover for Jubilee was the responsibility of **Air Vice-Marshal Trafford Leigh-Mallory**, Commander No. 11 Group, Fighter Command. Leigh-Mallory had served as a young subaltern during the First War where he was wounded at Ypres. In July 1916 he joined the fledgling Royal Flying Corps and remained an airman for the rest of his life. In 1919 he joined the Royal Air Force where he was a great advocate of air–ground co-operation. During the Battle of Britain he headed No. 12 Group in the Midlands, eventually taking over No. 11 Group from Air Vice-Marshal Dowding in December 1942.

Major-General John H. Roberts, Commander Canadian 2nd Infantry Division. Roberts was Military Force Commander for the Dieppe raid and controlled the whole of the land battle. His headquarters was located with the Naval Force Commander aboard the destroyer HMS *Calpe*. Located out to sea, he was always remote from what was happening on shore and did not immediately recognise the scale of the disaster that was unfolding. (Canada Dept of National Defence, National Archives of Canada PA-153531)

Air Vice-Marshal Trafford Leigh-Mallory, Air Force Commander for Jubilee. Leigh-Mallory headed No. 11 Group, Fighter Command, and brought together 67 RAF squadrons for the operation, hoping to bring the Luftwaffe to battle over the Channel and inflict a serious defeat on the enemy. (Imperial War Museum, CH11985)

GERMAN COMMANDERS

Generalfeldmarschall Gerd von Rundstedt, Commander in Chief West, controlled all occupation troops in North-West Europe from Holland to the Spanish border. He had 36 divisions at his disposal. Dieppe was in the sector of German Fifteenth Army, commanded by **Generaloberst Curt Haase**, which covered the coast from the Scheldt in Holland to Caen in Normandy. LXXXI Corps based in Rouen and commanded by 53-year-old **General der Panzertruppen Adolf Kuntzen**, was responsible for the defence of the stretch of coastline either side of Dieppe. **Generalleutnant Konrad Haase** aged 54 (no relation to the commander of Fifteenth Army) commanded German 302nd Infantry Division, which garrisoned Dieppe itself and the beaches either side. To differentiate between their army and division commanders, German troops nicknamed the divisional commander 'Der Kleine Haase' and the Fifteenth Army commander, 'Der Grosse Haase' ('Little Haase' and 'Big Haase').

OPPOSING ARMIES

The bulk of the troops allocated to the Dieppe raid were Canadian. The British Army provided two Commandos, the Royal Marines supplied a third and the American Army contributed a party of Rangers.

THE CANADIANS

During World War II, until January 1945, the Canadian Army in Europe was an all-volunteer service. None of the men who fought at Dieppe had been conscripted into serving overseas. On 1 September 1939 the Canadian Department of National Defence issued a General Order authorising the immediate organisation of a 'Canadian Active Service Force'. Two divisions supported by ancillary troops were raised, mainly from existing militia forces. These units included many famous militia regiments, each with a long history and numerous battle honours. The permanent Canadian Army was also enlarged through the mobilisation of citizen volunteers. No legislation was introduced for compulsory service in the armed forces.

The force attacking Dieppe included 50 American soldiers. These men came from the US 1st Ranger Battalion and joined various units in order to gain battle experience. It was also good propaganda for the Americans, for when news broke of the raid the newspapers in the USA were plastered with banner headlines proclaiming 'Yanks in 9-Hour Dieppe Raid'. This picture, taken after the operation, shows US Ranger Sergeant Alex Szima accepting a light from his comrade in arms Sergeant 'Bunny' Austin of 4 Commando. (Imperial War Museum, H22580)

The first troops from Canada to land in Britain were from the Canadian Active Service Force. On 17 December 1939 the advanced units of Canadian 1st Infantry Division landed in Greenock. Canadian 2nd Division followed in 1940, although not before several of its battalions had been sent for a period of garrison duty in Iceland. During 1940 two further divisions were raised in Canada destined for overseas service. With the collapse of France in June 1940 it became clear to the Canadian Government that its commitment to the British Commonwealth for the prosecution of the war would need to be considerably expanded. It was equally clear that this would be impossible with an all-volunteer force. Compulsory service would have to be introduced. In the summer of 1940 the National Resources Mobilisation Act was passed, conscripting men between the ages of 21 and 45. There was, however, no obligation for these conscripts to serve outside Canada. This remained the position until the act was amended in the summer of 1942, when the restriction on sending persons called up for military service out of the country was removed. This gave the Government full powers for general conscription, but these powers were not invoked until over two years later in November 1944, with the first compulsory conscripts arriving in Holland in January 1945. By the end of the war only 12,908 conscripts had been sent overseas out of a total commitment in Europe of 368,000 all ranks, giving the Canadians a 96.5 per cent all-volunteer army during World War II. It was a magnificent achievement.

Canadian 2nd Division, commanded by Major-General V.W. Odlum, arrived in Britain during the summer of 1940. Before all the division's constituent units could be concentrated three battalions, the Royal Regiment of Canada, Les Fusiliers Mont-Royal and the Cameron Highlanders of Ottawa, were sent to Iceland for garrison duties. They reinforced the small British contingent already on the island. Following the fall of France, Iceland was of great importance to the Allies. In German

Canadian troops going aboard two Landing Craft (Mechanised) MK 1 – LCM(1). This type of landing craft was capable of carrying a light tank, armoured car or transport up to 16 tons, or 100 troops. The craft in the foreground is loaded with a Universal Carrier, known more commonly as the Bren Carrier. This was one of the most widely used light AFVs of the war. (National Archives of Canada, PA-183767)

hands the island would have posed a threat to the sea lanes of the North Atlantic. Britain wanted all of 2nd Division to be concentrated there, but the Canadian Government felt that public opinion at home would object to Canadian forces being permanently in garrison abroad. Britain eventually concurred and the entire 2nd Division was landed in England to be replaced in Iceland by the British 49th (West Riding) Division.

The Canadian Army organisation, training, equipment and doctrine broadly conformed to that of the British Army. Like its British counterparts, Canadian 2nd Infantry Division consisted of three brigades (4th, 5th and 6th Brigades) of three infantry battalions, a machine gun battalion, three regiments of field artillery and other supporting arms. Canadian 4th Infantry Brigade included the Royal Regiment of Canada, the Royal Hamilton Light Infantry and the Essex Scottish Regiment; 5th Brigade consisted of the Black Watch of Canada, Le Régiment de Maisonneuve and the Calgary Highlanders, whilst 6th Brigade was made up of Les Fusiliers Mont-Royal, the Queen's Own Cameron Highlanders of Canada and the South Saskatchewan Regiment. Providing support were the Cameron Highlanders of Ottawa (machine gun battalion), the guns of the 4th, 5th and 6th Royal Canadian Artillery Field Regiments and the armoured cars of the 8th Reconnaissance Regiment (14th Canadian Hussars) together with Canadian engineers and signallers.

Major-General Odlum was replaced by MajGen John Hamilton Roberts as commander of 2nd Division late in 1941. Roberts had commanded the 1st Field Regiment in Canadian 1st Division during its brief spell in France in 1940 and evacuated the unit through Brest as that country fell to the German blitzkrieg. He took over the division and brought a new impetus to the training and performance of the unit. During the first two years the division spent in the UK, morale had dipped and discipline had become relaxed. It was inevitable after such a long period away from home, with nothing but the dull routine of individual training to fill each day, that troops had begun to question their role in the war. The weather during those two years was not to the troops' liking; winters were uncommonly harsh, cold and damp and the camps they were housed in were dreary and uncomfortable. Out of barracks the Commonwealth troops were unruly and often badly behaved, seeking some relief from homesickness and boredom in riotous behaviour. In the 20 months prior to Dieppe, the men of the 2nd Division committed a total of 21,492 listed offences.

Having inherited these problems, MajGen Roberts set about rectifying some of them. Many of the older officers were weeded out and given other jobs. The younger officers that replaced them gave the men new heart. Roberts organised a vigorous programme of exercises and manoeuvres into which the men's surplus energy could be channelled. Then, on 8 May 1942, came the news that the whole division had been waiting for. Training was to begin in earnest for a specific task – the division was to see action at last.

Roberts had selected the six battalions of 4th and 6th Brigades from his division to carry out the raid. By 20 May all of these units had arrived on the Isle of Wight to undergo specialised training in specific raiding tasks. The Isle of Wight was the perfect location for the amphibious training and landing exercises, which they began once the units had assembled. It was isolated from the mainland, allowing tight security to be maintained. It had numerous beaches ideal for practising landing

techniques and all around the island were stretches of high chalk cliffs similar to those at Dieppe. When the 5,000-strong detachment from the division had arrived on the island and joined with the naval and auxiliary forces required for the raid, the Isle of Wight was sealed; only those civilians who lived and worked there were allowed to remain. Then the training began in earnest.

The first thing was to improve the physical fitness of the troops. A programme of assault courses and speed marches strengthened their stamina, whilst sessions of bayonet practise, cliff climbing, weapons training, street fighting, landing craft embarkation and unarmed combat improved their ability. Training was hard, but little by little the force began to gain pride and belief in itself and in its proficiency. As the date for Operation Rutter approached, the division was fighting fit and ready for action. However, as noted above, Rutter was abandoned in early July so the attacking force left the Isle of Wight, not to assault Dieppe as intended, but to disperse back to camps in Sussex and Surrey. Although the raid, now renamed Jubilee, was back on and scheduled for 18–19 August, the troops whiled away their time oblivious to the fact until just before the operation was launched, when they were given a final briefing on their objectives and sent down to the ships.

COMMANDOS AND RANGERS

In Operation Jubilee the two brigades of 2nd Division were still to land over open beaches and carry out the main objectives of the raid, but the planning of the wide flanking attacks had changed. Airborne troops were no longer to capture the large German coastal batteries that overlooked the assault. The emplacements were now to be taken in a seaborne attack

Orange I Beach at Vasterival, landing place for Maj Mills-Roberts' party of 4 Commando. This modern picture shows the formidable cliffs and the two gullies that lead up from the beach, both of which were blocked by barbed wire and booby traps. The commandos made their exit from the beach up the right-hand gully. (Ken Ford)

by army Commandos. 4 Commando would assault the battery at Varengeville (Hess Battery) and 3 Commando would attack the guns at Berneval (Goebbels Battery). Both of these army Commandos had already seen action in the war and both were composed of volunteers. They now began a furious period of training to prepare them for their specific tasks.

The first nine Commandos had been raised in the summer of 1940, with the core of their numbers coming from the Independent Companies that had been formed to act as 'guerrillas' behind enemy lines. The original ten Independent Companies, each containing 20 officers and 270 men, had been established as ship-based forces intended to land in the rear of the enemy to harass communications and supply lines. The new Commandos were much larger than the Independent Companies, with around 24 officers and 435 other ranks. They were organised into one headquarters and five fighting Troops, each containing three officers and around 60 fighting men. Signallers and support facilities made up the remainder. They were formed to carry out a variety of tasks, but essentially their main role was to take the fight back to occupied Europe at a time when British land forces were unable to engage the enemy directly. Commando raiding parties were originally intended to undertake such tasks as general reconnaissance of enemy coasts, sabotage raids against enemy installations and to provide flank support for major incursions or attacks. These Commandos were highly trained specialised infantry, lightly armed and flexibly organised. They were extremely fit and capable of executing swift attacks over ground from which none was expected. Their combat role was as a 'hit and run' force, targeted on a specific objective; they were not intended to be used as frontline infantry.

3 Commando was raised in July 1940 under LtCol J.F. Durnford-Slater and was later involved in raids on Guernsey, the Lofoten Islands and Vaagsö. 4 Commando, commanded by LtCol The Lord Lovat, was established at the same time and participated in the Lofoten attack in December 1941. It also provided parties of its men for other raids such as that against the docks at St Nazaire. Both of these Commandos were purpose-built for the roles assigned to them. They now spent a period of time perfecting their skills and finalising a plan for the capture of the batteries.

Durnford-Slater's Commando moved from Scotland to Seaford in Sussex, whilst Lord Lovat took 4 Commando down to Weymouth. Intelligence reports and reconnaissance photographs were studied and once a plan of attack had been devised, the Commandos simulated the assaults over and over again. Each day started with a five-mile speed-march with full equipment, the Commando carrying everything they might need during the raid, gradually improving the time taken until the march could be completed in just 45 minutes. Demolition programmes were organised, with each man becoming competent not only in his own task, but also that of others to ensure that tasks were still carried out in the event of casualties. Lovat's men practised in Lulworth Cove in Dorset, including eight full-scale rehearsals of their proposed landings. 3 Commando rehearsed coming ashore beneath the chalk cliffs of the Sussex Downs, landing at dawn from tiny assault craft after circling the Isle of Wight all night. As mid-August approached, the two Commandos were fully trained and raring to go.

Attached to Mountbatten's Combined Operations HQ at that time was a group of American officers hoping to gain experience of raiding and invasion techniques. Senior amongst these was Brigadier General Lucian Truscott who had recently formed the first American 'Commandos' which he called Rangers. The US 1st Ranger Battalion had been raised in June 1942 with volunteers from those American troops who had already arrived in Northern Ireland. Truscott created this Ranger force along similar lines to the British Commandos. The initial recruits undertook the same punishing training regime at the Commando Basic Training Centre at Achnacarry in Scotland and worked on the same raiding techniques. Mountbatten now asked Truscott whether he would like some Rangers to participate in the raid in order to give them an insight into battle conditions. Truscott readily agreed and nominated six officers and 44 other ranks to accompany the Jubilee force.

Queens Own Cameron Highlanders of Canada disembarking from a landing ship infantry (LSI) onto assault landing craft (LCA) ready for the attack. These LCAs could carry 30 fully loaded men. Fine weather and calm seas aided the process and there was none of the seasickness amongst the troops that marred the later D-Day landings in Normandy. (National Archives of Canada, PA-113245)

ORDER OF BATTLE

MILITARY FORCE COMMANDER – MajGen John Hamilton Roberts

Canadian 4th Infantry Brigade   **Brig Sherwood Lett**
Royal Regiment of Canada   LtCol Cato
Royal Hamilton Light Infantry   LtCol Labatt
Essex Scottish Regiment   LtCol Jasperson

Canadian 6th Infantry Brigade   **Brig William Southam**
Fusiliers Mont Royal   LtCol Menard
Cameron Highlanders of Canada   LtCol Gostling
South Saskatchewan Regiment   LtCol Merritt

Canadian 14th Tank Battalion (Calgary Tanks)   LtCol Andrews

British 3 Commando   LtCol Durnford-Slater
British 4 Commando   LtCol The Lord Lovat
Royal Marine A Commando   LtCol Picton-Phillips

Naval Force Commander   **Capt John Hughes-Hallett**

Destroyers
HMS *Calpe* (HQ Ship)   LtCdr Wallace
HMS *Fernie*   Lt Willett
HMS *Brocklesby*   LtCdr Pumphrey
HMS *Garth*   LtCdr Scatchard
HMS *Albrighton*   LtCdr Hanson
HMS *Berkeley*   Lt Yorke
HMS *Bleasdale*   Lt North-Lewis
ORP *Slazak*   Cdr Tyminiski

Sloop and Gunboat
HMS *Alresford*   Cdr Dunbar
HMS *Locust*   LtCdr Stride

Minesweeper Flotillas
9th Minesweeping Flotilla   Cdr Rust
13th Minesweeping Flotilla   Cdr Ede

Landing Ships
HMS *Glengyle* (LSI Large)   Capt McGrath
HMS *Queen Emma* (LSI Medium)   Capt Gibbs
HMS *Princess Beatrix* (LSI Medium)   Cdr Brunton
HMS *Prince Charles* (LSI Small)   Cdr Dennis
HMS *Prince Albert* (LSI Small)   Cdr Peate
HMS *Prince Leopold* (LSI Small)   LtCdr Byles
HMS *Princess Astrid* (LSI Small)   LtCdr Hall
HMS *Invicta* (LSI Small)   Cdr Robertson
HMS *Duke of Wellington* (LSI Small)   LtCdr Coombes

Landing Craft from the LSIs consisted of:
60 Landing Craft Assault (LCA)
8 Landing Craft Support (LCS)
7 Landing Craft Mechanised (LCM)

First Flotilla Group 5 (Yellow Beach)   **Lt Stevens**
LCPs No: 1, 80, 81, 85, 86, 87, 95, 118, 128, 145, 157

Second Flotilla Group 6 (Green Beach)   **Lt Byerley**
LCPs No: 19, 88, 94, 119, 124, 125, 129, 147, 156

Fourth Flotilla Group 7 (Floating Reserve)   **Lt Wallace**
LCPs No: 28, 53, 170, 172, 173, 174, 175, 186, 187, 188, 192, 195, 199, 212

Fifth Flotilla Group 7 (Floating Reserve)   **LtCdr Roulston**
LCPs No: 31, 45, 155, 163, 165, 166, 167, 208, 209, 210, 614

Sixth Flotilla Group 6 (Green Beach)　　　　　　　Lt Murray
LCPs No: 127, 130, 131, 132, 134, 135, 136, 153, 158

Seventh Flotilla Group 6 (Green Beach)　　　　　LtCdr Garrard
LCPs No: 83, 84, 99, 101, 102, 104, 110, 113, 159, 160

Twenty-fourth Flotilla Group 5 (Yellow Beach)　　LtCdr Corke
LCPs No: 3, 4, 13, 15, 23, 24, 34, 40, 41, 42, 43, 44, 78, 115

Second Landing Craft Tank (LCT) Flotilla　　　　LtCdr Brownell[1]
LCTs No: 121, 124, 125, 126, 127, 145, 163, 165, 166, 169

First Landing Craft Flak (LCF) Flotilla　　　　　LtCdr Brownell
LCF(L)s No: 1, 2, 3, 4, 5, 6

Fourth Landing Craft Tank (LCT) Flotilla　　　　LtCdr Masterman
LCTs No: 302, 303, 304, 305, 306, 307, 308, 309, 310, 318, 325, 360, 361, 376.

Escorting Craft
Motor Gun Boats (MGB) No: 50, 51, 52, 57, 312, 315, 316, 317, 320, 321, 323, 326
Steam Gun Boats (SGB) No: 5, 6, 8, 9
Motor Launches (ML) No: 114, 120, 123, 171, 187, 189, 190, 191, 193, 194, 208, 214, 230, 246,
　　291, 292, 309, 343, 344, 346
Free French Chasseurs No: 5, 10, 13, 14, 41, 42, 43

AIR FORCE COMMANDER　　　　　　**Air Vice-Marshal Trafford Leigh-Mallory**

Royal Air Force Fighter Command No 11 Group
Spitfire Squadrons
19, 41, 64, 65, 66, 71, 81, 91, 111, 118, 121, 122, 124, 129, 130, 131, 133, 154, 165, 222, 232,
242, 302, 303, 306, 307, 308, 309, 310, 312, 317, 331, 332, 340, 350, 401, 402, 403, 411, 412,
416, 485, 501, 602, 610, 611, 616.

Hurricane Squadrons
3, 32, 43, 87, 174, 175, 245, 253.

Typhoon Squadrons
56, 266, 609.

Boston Squadrons
88, 107, 226, 418, 605.

Blenheim Squadrons
13, 614.

Mustang Squadrons
26, 239, 400, 414.

Beaufighter Squadron
141.

USAAF 97th Bombardment Group
B-17 Squadrons
340th, 341st, 342nd, 414th.

---

　1 Also CO of LCF Flotilla

Green Beach at Pourville where the South Saskatchewan Regiment came ashore. This modern view was taken from the site of the German radar station. As with all of the beaches chosen for the raid, the landing site was overlooked by enemy-held high ground. (Ken Ford)

THE GERMANS

The bulk of the German Army in 1942, most especially its elite units, was serving on the Eastern Front against the Soviet Red Army. After the victorious French campaign and the eviction of the British Expeditionary Force from the Continent, the role of the German army in the west was one of occupation and defence. The conquered territories having been subdued, they were now garrisoned by second line static troops, allowing the cream of the German fighting forces to be transferred to the Eastern Front, which was consuming men and materiel in vast quantities.

The top of the gully leading up from Yellow I Beach at Berneval. Two parties from 3 Commando came up this re-entrant through wire and mined obstacles, only to be forced back down again by enemy counterattacks. In the centre is a monument commemorating the landing, surrounded with wreaths laid during the ceremonies that marked the 60th anniversary of the raid in 2002. (Ken Ford)

Guarding the 50 miles of coastline either side of Dieppe and garrisoning the town and the countryside around the port was the German 302nd Infantry Division commanded by GenLt Konrad Haase. The division had been formed in Germany in December 1940, one of nine new divisions raised during Mobilisation Wave 13, specifically tasked with occupation duties in Western Europe. Its came from Wehrkreis II, the military district headquartered in Stettin in northern Germany and its men came from the surrounding regions of Mecklenburg and Pomerania. The division comprised three regiments, 570th, 571st and 572nd Infantry Regiments, each containing two battalions. The 302nd Artillery Regiment, 302nd Reconnaissance Battalion, 302nd Anti-tank Battalion, 302nd Engineer Battalion and 302nd Signal Battalion provided supporting arms.

The division arrived in the area in April 1941, after spending a short time on garrison duties in Germany. At the time Haase's division was at full strength and fully equipped. It soon settled into occupation duties and Haase organised his men to police the local population and defend the locality. However, the situation did not remain stable for long. The flow of new recruits from the military districts of the Reich proved inadequate to replace the vast losses suffered in the bitter fighting in the east. In an attempt to halt the steady attrition of German forces in Russia troops were stripped from established divisions in the field. Little by little, 302nd Division was robbed of its German nationals and replaced with foreign conscripts, many of whom were less than enthusiastic servants of the Reich. Poles, Czechs, Belgians and even Russians joined the ranks of the division defending Dieppe.

302nd Division was, in every way, a second rate unit. The expertise of its personnel varied and many of the rank and file were of questionable quality, as was its equipment. Much modern weaponry was commandeered for Russia and obsolete replacements supplied. Much of its artillery was foreign and pre-war, captured during campaigns in Czechoslovakia, France and Russia. Even salvaged British weapons were pressed into service. Understandably, such a motley assortment of weapons, and a relative shortage of ammunition for them, further exacerbated supply difficulties. Most transport was horse-drawn, supplemented by bicycles, with French trucks acquired to pull artillery and heavy equipment. However, static troops with an exclusively defensive role do not necessarily need the best weaponry. In formidable concrete fortifications and armed with even out-of-date machine guns, the poorest troops could give a good account of themselves.

OPPOSING PLANS

ALLIED PLANNING

The raid on Dieppe had many objectives. It resulted first and foremost from the political pressure to make some sort of demonstration to help relieve pressure on the hard-pressed Red Army. The Allies, and more specifically the British, had to be seen to be taking the fight to Nazi-occupied Europe. The raid would also allow the Canadians to gain battle experience. It was important for the morale of the Canadian troops themselves, and for that on the home front in Canada, to demonstrate that they could and would make a demonstrable contribution to the war effort. The raid was also a test of the degree to which co-operation between the individual service arms could be achieved. Was it possible to coordinate army, navy and air force assets to transport, protect and land a large amphibious force? The 'reconnaissance in force' would allow the strength of the defences of an occupied German port to be assessed and the means by which to overcome them to be developed. It was also hoped that the now elusive Luftwaffe could be brought to battle in the skies above Dieppe and considerable losses in men and aircraft inflicted upon it. The success or failure of Operation Jubilee would shape future decisions, both strategic and tactical, on the nature and direction of the plans for the ultimate opening of the second front.

Boston aircrews of an RAF bomber squadron relax before taking off on their own mission to Dieppe. The RAF flew 2,614 sorties over the battle area during the operation, resulting in the loss of 106 aircraft and the deaths of 67 pilots. (Imperial War Museum, CH 6529)

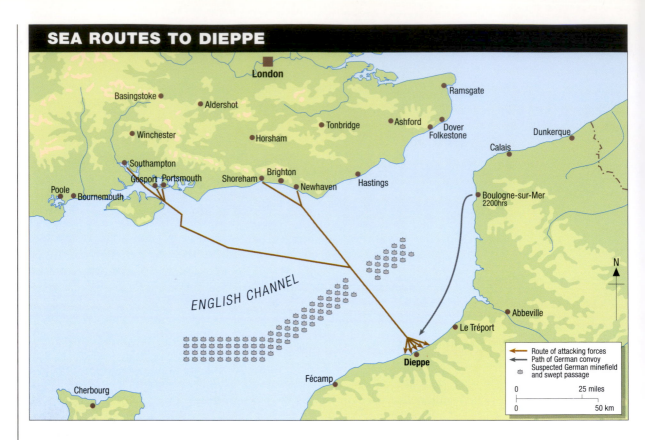

SEA ROUTES TO DIEPPE

The Canadian Targets

The two assault brigades of Canadian 2nd Division were given a number of objectives during the raid. They would land on three separate beaches and link up to form an integrated lodgement. Tanks would land at Dieppe and join with infantry to strike inland and capture the airfield to the south of the town and the German divisional headquarters that was thought to be in the area. Engineer and demolition parties would sabotage dock installations, the telephone exchange, railways, marshalling yards, tunnels, the gas works and the power station, whilst others tried to capture information, documents and communication devices. The radar site at Pourville was a particularly important target; special groups of infantry were briefed both to eliminate its operation and to capture any secret radar equipment. A party of Royal Marines landing with the Canadians in Dieppe would capture and remove to England invasion barges and other craft that were in the harbour. Beach defences were to be inspected, tactical layouts examined and enemy deployment monitored. There were great lessons to be learned and much information to be gained from the attack. This raid was about much more than just inflicting casualties on the Germans.

The port of Dieppe is situated astride the estuary of the River Arques. The river has created a valley less than a mile wide at its mouth, dominated by high chalk headlands on either side. Between these headlands lies the town and harbour of Dieppe, with a steep shingle beach along the seafront. High white cliffs stretch into the distance to the east and west of the town.

Eight landing beaches had been identified for the raid. On the extreme left and right flanks, each Commando was allocated two small beaches from which to assault the coastal batteries codenamed 'Hess'

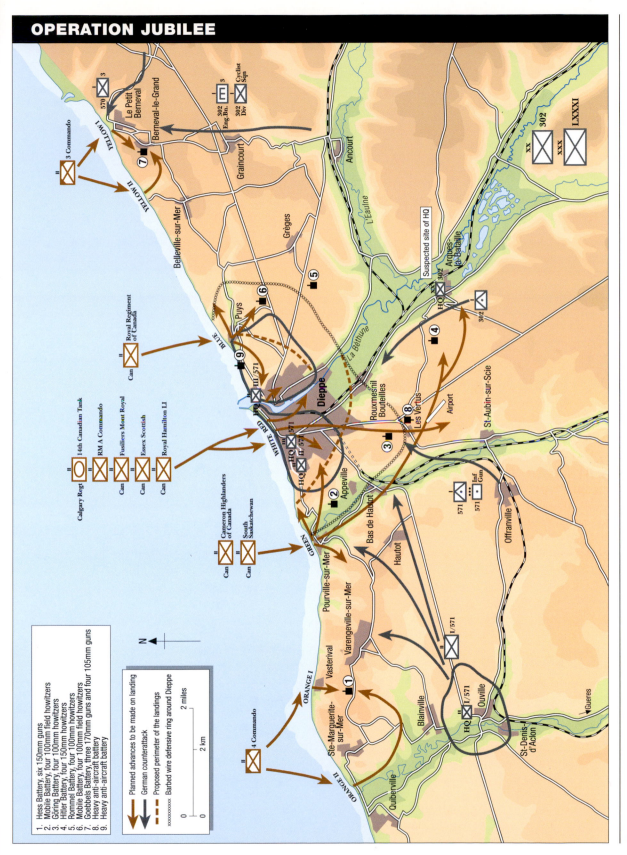

Le Petit
Berneval

570 ³

Berneval-le-Grand

E ³
302   Cyclist
Eng.Bn.   Sqn
302
Div

3 Commando

Graincourt

Ancourt

302

LXXXI

1 MOTEL

YELLOW I

II MOTEL

7

Belleville-sur-Mer

Gréges

L'Eauline

Suspected site of HQ

Arques-
la-Bataille

302

5

Royal Regiment
of Canada

6

Puys

BLUE

Can

La Béthune

302

HQ

4

9

III/ 571

St-Aubin-sur-Scie

14th Canadian Tank

RM A Commando

Fusiliers Mont Royal

Essex Scottish

Royal Hamilton LI

Calgary Regt

Can

Can

Can

WHITE

RED

Dieppe

Rouxmesnil
Bouteilles

8

Les Vertus

Airport

HQ II/ 571

3

HQ II/ 571

Appeville

2

Cameron Highlanders
of Canada

South
Saskatchewan

Can

Can

GREEN

Bas de Hautot

571   571   Offranville

Inf   Gun

Pourville-sur-Mer

Hautot

Varengeville-sur-Mer

I/ 571

Vasterival

ORANGE I

1

Ste-Marguerite-
sur-Mer

Blainville

HQ I/ 571

Ouville

St-Denis-
d'Aclon

Guéres

4 Commando

Quiberville

ORANGE II

N

Legend:
1. Hess Battery, six 150mm guns
2. Mobile Battery, four 100mm field howitzers
3. Göring Battery, four 100mm howitzers
4. Hitler Battery, four 150mm howitzers
5. Rommel Battery, four 100mm howitzers
6. Mobile Battery, four 100mm field howitzers
7. Goebbels Battery, three 170mm guns and four 105mm guns
8. Heavy anti-aircraft battery
9. Heavy anti-aircraft battery

Planned advances to be made on landing

German counterattack

Proposed perimeter of the landings

xxxxxxxxxxxxxx Barbed wire defensive ring around Dieppe

2 miles

2 km

0

0

31

A view of White and Red Beaches at Dieppe from the top of a German bunker. The armoured cupola on this emplacement dates from after 1942, but the site demonstrates the commanding view over the landing beaches which the Germans had. (Ken Ford)

and 'Goebbels'. On the extreme west of the proposed lodgement, 4 Commando would come ashore on Orange I and II Beaches at Vasterival and Quiberville; on the easternmost flank 3 Commando would arrive over Yellow I and II Beaches at Berneval and Belleville-sur-Mer. In the centre, Dieppe's town beach was split into two, with the westerly landing point called White Beach and the easterly one labelled Red Beach. The next beach to the east of Dieppe was at Puys, this was designated Blue Beach, whilst on the other side of Dieppe to the west, Green Beach was at Pourville.

The plan called for the main attack to be launched directly onto the town beach in the centre of Dieppe. Two battalions of Canadian 4th Infantry Brigade, commanded by Brigadier Sherwood Lett, would land abreast: the Essex Scottish on the left on Red Beach, the Royal Hamilton Light Infantry on the right on White Beach. Arriving with the assault waves, landing craft tank (LCT) would beach with the Churchill tanks of the Canadian 14th Tank Battalion, the Calgary Regiment. Tanks and infantry would then attack and hold the town. Engineer and

Blue Beach at Puys. A modern picture taken from alongside the high sea wall where so many men of the Royal Regiment of Canada were killed. Close to the white house at the top of the hill are the two pillboxes that contained the machine guns that caused such carnage during the landings. It was very difficult to find any cover from this fire anywhere on the beach. (Ken Ford)

demolition units would also land to carry out their tasks. The brigade's other battalion, the Royal Regiment of Canada, would land a mile to the east of Dieppe at Puys. Its troops would then attack over the headland between the two beaches and link up with the Essex Scottish in Dieppe, whilst a party of the Royal Regiment attacked a German field battery codenamed 'Rommel' behind the town.

Canadian 6th Brigade's assault was aimed at Green Beach at Pourville. The brigade was commanded by Brigadier W. Southam and his lead battalion, the South Saskatchewan Regiment, was to land first and secure a beachhead astride the River Scie. The main body of South Sasketchewans would then swing to the left and take the radar station, the strongpoint of Quatre Vents Farm and the western headland overlooking Dieppe to link up with the Royal Hamilton Light Infantry, whilst the balance of the battalion seized the high ground to the west of Pourville. Following behind the assault battalion, the Queen's Own Cameron Highlanders of Canada would land at Pourville and strike southwards along the eastern bank of the River Scie towards the airfield at St Aubin. It would link up en route with the second wave of tanks that was to land at Dieppe. Together they would seize the airfield, attack the German divisional HQ thought to be at Arques-la-Bataille and eliminate the nearby German artillery battery codenamed 'Hitler'. 6th Brigade's third battalion, Les Fusiliers Mont-Royal, was to be held as the division's floating reserve and to be landed wherever it was needed.

The landings were timed to take place at dawn. The flank attacks by the Commandos were to go in first at 0450hrs. This was nautical twilight when the sun was still 12° below the horizon but with enough faint light available to discern landmarks. The main assault would take place at civil twilight, when the sun is just 6° below the horizon at 0520hrs, in effect at daybreak. Sunrise was at 0550hrs.

On the extreme flanks, Lovat's 4 Commando would land in two groups on Orange I and II Beaches at 0450hrs. The group from Orange I Beach at Vasterival would advance directly towards Hess Battery and engage it with small arms and mortar fire, whilst the larger second group, commanded by Lord Lovat, landed at Quiberville and carried out a wide flanking movement to assault the battery from the rear. At the same time on the extreme east of the proposed lodgement, Durnford-Slater's 3 Commando would carry out similar attacks on the Goebbels Battery via landings on Yellow I and II Beaches at Berneval and Belleville-sur-Mer.

The Naval Plans

Captain John Hughes-Hallett, Naval Force Commander, had 237 craft at his disposal for the operation. At first, this might seem to be a very large fleet, but most of them were light vessels or landing craft. The only real firepower with which to protect the ships and bombard the enemy shore was from the 4in. guns of eight destroyers and one gunboat. The weapons carried on the other craft ranged from the 3in. guns of the steam gunboats to light cannons such as the 40mm and 20mm Bofors and Oerlikons of the support vessels. This lack of firepower from the sea was a crucial mistake. The 4in. naval guns could do little damage to heavily protected defensive emplacements, but would serve merely to force the German defenders to keep their heads down. Mountbatten had asked for a powerful battleship to accompany the raid to engage

Orange II Beach at Quiberville, the landing place of Lord Lovat's party from 4 Commando. The main opposition to the landing came not from enemy on the high ground but from two pillboxes near the beach. Once ashore, Lovat's commandos moved eastwards to attack Hess Battery. The landing craft then withdrew to wait off Orange I Beach for the order to evacuate the whole Commando after the raid was over. (Ken Ford)

shore targets with weight and precision, but the Admiralty were terrified of losing a capital ship to German air attacks and swiftly rejected the request. It was decided to leave it to the RAF to shatter the enemy defences with a heavy aerial bombardment prior to the landings.

Captain Hughes Hallett decided that as the troops taking part in Jubilee were already trained and dispersed, the seaborne operation could be mounted differently from that for Rutter. He wanted to avoid the likelihood of the force being detected and attacked by German aircraft. He felt there was no longer a need for the ships to be concentrated as they had been before. The various units involved could now move directly from their assembly points to nearby ports of embarkation and sail the evening they boarded. Further dispersion could be obtained by sending certain

The Headquarters ship HMS *Calpe* seen laying smoke off Dieppe during the operation. The *Calpe* was the communications centre for the raid and had the Naval Force Commander, Capt Hughes-Hallett, and the Military Force Commander, MajGen Roberts on board. (Canada Dept of Military Defence/National Archives Canada, PA-116291)

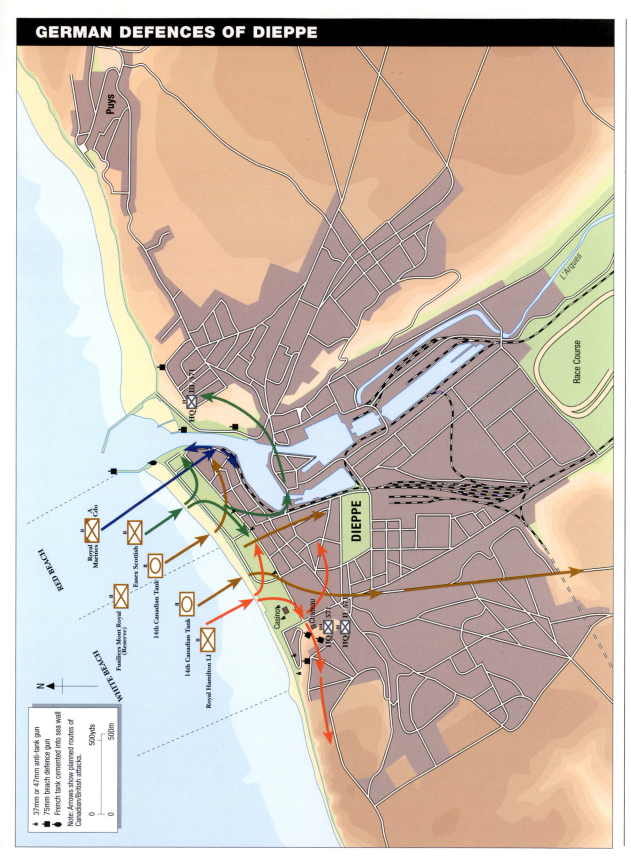

GERMAN DEFENCES OF DIEPPE

Puys

L'Arques

Race Course

DIEPPE

HQ III, 571

Casino

Château

HQ I, 571

HQ II, 571

RED BEACH

WHITE BEACH

A Cdo
Royal Marines

Essex Scottish

Fusiliers Mont Royal (Reserve)

14th Canadian Tank

14th Canadian Tank

Royal Hamilton LI

N

37mm or 47mm anti-tank gun
75mm beach defence gun
French tank cemented into sea wall

Note: Arrows show planned routes of Canadian/British attacks.

500yds
500m

0
0

The view from the cockpit of Flight Lieutenant Andrews' Hurricane fighter-bomber as he strafed a German gun position at Dieppe on the morning of the raid. (Imperial War Museum, C3197)

troops direct from England in their landing craft, avoiding the need for them to be transhipped from landing ships to assault craft. Jubilee was to be launched from a variety of south coast ports, each flotilla's departure and passage timed so as to bring the force together off the French coast at the appropriate moment.

Ships would be embarking from Southampton, Portsmouth, Gosport, Shoreham and Newhaven. The passage was to be made in darkness, but those from Southampton would have to leave whilst it was still light to make the longer journey. To avoid enemy detection, the vessels were to be elaborately disguised to resemble a coastal convoy. The various groups would later assemble near the French coast and be escorted through a German minefield to their respective lowering points ready to make their individual runs to the beaches.

The RAF's Plan

One of the first things that was abandoned during the planning stages was the high-level night bombing of Dieppe prior to the raid. The Air Force Commander was of the opinion that it was not the best way to use the bombers and such a raid would put the enemy on alert. The Military Force Commander was also of the opinion that it was not a good idea because the destruction of large numbers of buildings would block the streets with rubble making them impassable to tanks. As an alternative, Air Marshal Leigh-Mallory proposed that diversionary bombing attacks would be made on German airfields in northern France and that cannon-firing fighters would attack the German beach defences and the high ground on either side of Dieppe just before the landings. Hurricane fighter-bombers would also attack individual targets with 250lb bombs. The great pre-assault bombardment guaranteed to flatten German defences had now been reduced to fighter-bomber raids by Hurricanes and light selected gunfire from small destroyers.

During the planning for Jubilee the RAF was always seen as having two main objectives in the operation: first, they were to provide air cover for the attacking forces and, second, they were to attack the enemy's defensive capability. But the size of the seaborne operation allowed

Leigh-Mallory to contemplate another objective. He intended to throw down the gauntlet to the Luftwaffe and entice it into battle. It was likely that as the landings developed the Germans might well regard them as the prelude to an invasion, or at least that the Allies were trying to carve out a beachhead in France. The Luftwaffe would in all likelihood bring into the attack all the aircraft it could muster. If that was the case, the RAF wanted to be ready for them. At his disposal for Jubilee Leigh-Mallory had 68 squadrons, a force greater than any available to Air Chief Marshal Dowding at any one time during the Battle of Britain two years previously. The RAF fully intended to take on the Luftwaffe at Dieppe and beat it.

GERMAN PLANS

At the time of the assault, Dieppe had been in German hands for over two years. Not unnaturally, the enemy had taken steps to defend it. The stretch of coastline 50 miles either side of Dieppe was assigned to the German 302nd Division. Its task was a defensive one, garrisoning the area and waiting to repel any attack. Landings could only be made where the high chalk cliffs dipped down to the sea and fixed defences were naturally concentrated in these areas. The beaches were blocked with wire and often mined. Machine-guns mounted in concrete pillboxes covered every angle of the shore. Exits from the beaches were often via very steep gullies that could be further barred by concrete, wire and booby traps. Circling the landward side of Dieppe itself, a defensive perimeter of wire, roadblocks and pillboxes threw a continuous cordon around the town. Within this cordon were three field batteries of 4in. or 5.9in. guns, with two further batteries just outside this perimeter. On the headlands overlooking the town's beach and in the town itself were eight 75mm guns. The streets leading inland from the beach were blocked by concrete walls and covered by more weapons. The beach was bordered by two separate barbed wire entanglements, one on the shingle and another, seven feet thick, along the low sea wall. Machine-guns and light anti-aircraft guns were dotted along the esplanade and headlands. Pillboxes at either end of the seafront held more weapons. To the right of the grassy promenade between the beach and the town was the Casino, a large derelict building, reinforced for defence, containing more weapons covering the landing places. Also supporting the firepower of the 302nd Division in Dieppe was a naval unit equipped with eight 37mm anti-tank guns and two heavy Luftwaffe anti-aircraft batteries.

Further out from the port, to the extreme right and left of Dieppe, the large coastal gun batteries of Hess and Goebbels covered the sea approaches with their combined firepower of ten 150mm weapons. These guns were the responsibility of the navy and were manned by naval detachments. They were both sited well outside the Dieppe defence zone and GenLt Haase's forces were too stretched elsewhere to provide the necessary infantry to protect them. Before the raid there had been several acrimonious exchanges between the army and the navy about the exposed position of the guns and their vulnerability, but although some agreement was eventually reached about repositioning the weapons, no action was taken before the raid.

GenLt Konrad Haase, Commander 302nd Division, had given the task of defending the actual town of Dieppe to Oberstleutnant Hermann Bartelt's 571st Regiment. Bartelt's HQ was located in the Château overlooking the main beach in Dieppe. The two depleted battalions of his regiment consisted of just 1,500 men. These were thinly spread from Varengeville in the west to Berneval in the east, leaving entire areas short of troops. At Puys, a garrison of just 50 men guarded the beach, whilst on the seafront at Dieppe a company of 150 men held the mile long stretch of beach.

Although the coastal area around Dieppe was thinly held by second-rate troops, when combined with machine-guns and concrete fortifications this represented a formidable obstacle to any assault. The defence of such a long front inevitably meant that it would be lightly held, but German planning accommodated this by having strong reserves available inland. Half of Haase's force was in reserve, with both Corps (four rifle battalions at Duclair) and army (10th Panzer Division at Amiens) reserves available within 50 miles.

Landing craft personnel (LCP) begin the long run into the beaches during the attack. Smoke generators helped cover their progress until they were very close to the shore. (National Archives of Canada, PA-183770)

THE FLANK ATTACKS

During the evening of 18 August, Lord Lovat's 4 Commando embarked at Southampton in the infantry landing ship (LSI) *Prince Albert*, a converted, pre-war, cross-Channel ferry. Also sailing from Southampton were the South Saskatchewans and the Royal Hamilton Light Infantry in the LSIs *Princess Beatrix*, *Invicta* and *Glengyle*. The Essex Scottish Regiment was split into two groups, one of which left Southampton in the *Prince Leopold*, the other from Portsmouth in the *Prince Charles*.

Portsmouth was also the embarkation port for the Royal Marine A Commando, commanded by LtCol Joseph Picton-Phillips. Part of Phillips' force sailed in seven 'Chasseurs' of the Free French Navy. The crews of these small coastal craft of 150 tons had brought them to British ports after the fall of France in 1940. They were armed with a 75mm gun and two heavy machine-guns. The remainder of the Royal Marine Commando, together with its commander, embarked on HMS *Locust*, a 500-ton river gunboat armed with one 4in. gun and one 3.7in. howitzer, whose shallow draught would allow it to come close inshore. Portsmouth was also the port of embarkation for the men of the Royal Regiment of Canada who boarded the LSIs *Queen Emma* and *Princess Astrid* to start their fateful journey towards Blue Beach at Puys. Across the harbour from Portsmouth, half of the Churchill tanks of the Canadian 14th Tank Battalion (Calgary Tanks) were loaded onto landing craft tank (LCT) from the hards at Gosport, the remainder were embarked from Newhaven.

Douglas Boston aircraft of the RAF completes a bombing run during Operation Jubilee. Smoke can be seen rising from Dieppe in the background. These light bombers made many sorties during the raid, the first of which were the attacks against German artillery batteries. They were later involved with laying and maintaining a smoke screen to help cover the withdrawal of troops from the beaches. (National Archives of Canada, PA-183771)

A Hunt-class destroyer opens fire on enemy defences at Dieppe. Fire from these 4in. guns had little effect on many of the well-concealed gun emplacements and bunkers, but it did serve to keep the German defenders under cover whilst the assaulting troops landed on the beaches. (National Archives of Canada, PA-183772)

In contrast to the relative comfort experienced by the troops who sailed from Southampton and Portsmouth in ships, those who left from the Sussex ports had a more cramped and exposed crossing to France. Durnford-Slater's 3 Commando embarked from Newhaven loaded into 23 landing craft personnel (LCP) that would carry them across the Channel right onto Yellow I and II Beaches. Also taking the same type of passage from Newhaven in LCPs were the Cameron Highlanders of Canada. The small wooden assault craft were known as 'Eurekas'. They held 25 troops in very uncomfortable and cramped conditions, but they were light and fast and relatively quiet, and would take troops right onto the beaches without having to be transhipped from larger vessels off the French coast. The floating reserve for the assault, Les Fusiliers Mont-Royal, were likewise conveyed from Shoreham in Sussex aboard a flotilla of LCPs.

Protecting the various convoys during the passage were eight Hunt-class destroyers: the headquarters ship *Calpe*, the *Fernie*, *Albrighton*, *Berkeley*, *Bleasdale*, *Brocklesby* and the *Garth*, together with the Polish destroyer *Slazak*. In addition, there were the gunboat *Locust*, the sloop *Alresford* and four steam gunboats, SGB5, SGB6, SGB8 and SGB9. Each of the latter was armed with one 3in. gun, two 2-pdr guns and two 20mm cannon.

YELLOW BEACH

The passage of the assault force across the Channel and through the minefield was uneventful. All was quiet until the leading ships approached the enemy coast, then, at 0347hrs, whilst between seven and eight miles out from shore, the extreme left of the armada had the misfortune to run into a number of enemy ships. Furthest to port was the steam gunboat SGB5, which was carrying the flotilla leader Commander Wyburd, LtCol Durnford-Slater and the leader of the US Rangers, Captain Roy Murray. It observed a line of ships off the port bow. The craft carrying 3 Commando had sailed right into the path of a German convoy of five small coasters and three escort vessels out of Boulogne heading for Dieppe. Almost

LCPs carrying infantry towards the beaches. As it is now very light, these are probably the Floating Reserve, Les Fusiliers Mont-Royal, heading for Red and White Beaches in Dieppe. The battalion was carried over the Channel in LCPs. (National Archives of Canada, PA113246)

immediately a star shell illuminated the sky exposing the collection of small craft. Within seconds, five German ships opened fire on the gunboat. SGB5 returned this fire but was unable to engage all of the vessels in action against it. Nearby escort vessels joined in the fight, with landing craft flak LCF(L)1 and motor launch ML346 joining in the action. Commander Wyburd decided to press on through the fire with his flotilla and remain on course for the Yellow Beaches. He signalled to the rest of the landing craft to make speed, convinced that any alteration to course would lead to complete disorganisation and render a successful landing impossible. Most of the German ships continued to concentrate their fire on the gunboat and she began to take serious damage. Small shells raked her sides and cannon fire splintered her decks. She was hit five times in her boilers and all her guns were put out of action. Her wireless was destroyed and 40 per cent of those on board became casualties, but Wyburd pressed resolutely on through the encounter and away from the enemy. ML346 was also hit several times and lost contact with the main group. LCF(L)1 continued engaging the enemy. For the next hour she fought a running battle with the German convoy even though her fire control was soon disabled. LCF(L)1 set one enemy ship on fire and sunk another, allowing the bulk of 3 Commando's flotilla to escape. At the end of the fight when the enemy withdrew to the refuge of Dieppe harbour, LCF(L)1 had suffered numerous hits, by which time many of her crew, including all her officers, had been killed or wounded.

The loss of communications on Wyburd's SGB5 meant it was impossible to summon the two protecting destroyers, *Slazak* and *Brocklesby*, who were just four miles away to the north-east. Their crews saw the action, but thought that the firing was coming from shore and did nothing. SGB5 had meanwhile pressed on towards the shore away from the enemy only to find that its little flotilla of landing craft had dispersed. The engagement with the German convoy had caused the 19 LCPs carrying the Commandos to

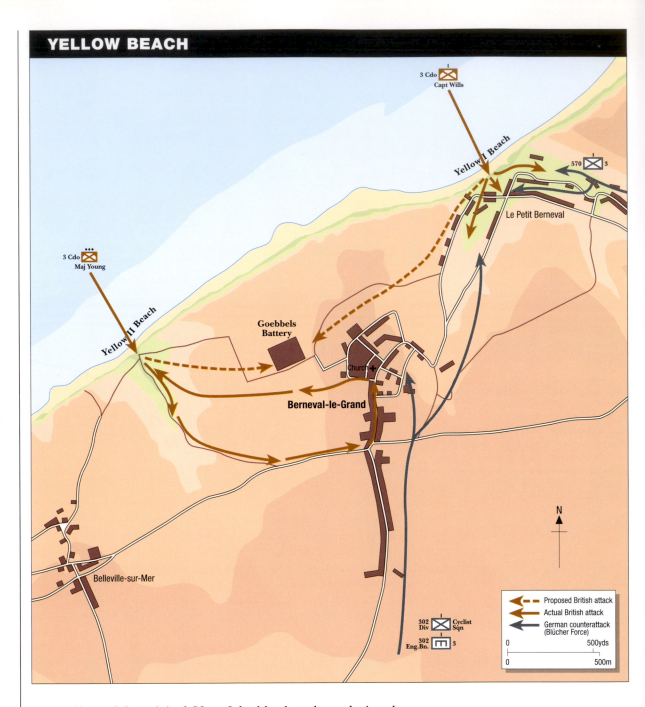

scatter (four of the original 23 craft had broken down during the voyage and had already returned to Newhaven). Of the remainder, four were damaged in the action and turned for home, three had remained with LCF(L)1 and five were still close by SGB5. The other seven had disappeared.

Commander Wyburd and LtCol Durnford-Slater both thought that circumstances were such that the original plan could not now be implemented. Their gunboat was dead in the water and their attacking force amounted to just five LCPs. They were unable to communicate by radio with the Naval and Military Force Commanders aboard the HQ ship HMS *Calpe* and so they agreed between themselves that the landings on Yellow Beaches should be abandoned. The two men transferred to an LCP and set off to find the HQ destroyer and report the bad news to Capt Hughes-Hallet and MajGen Roberts in person. But, far from being lost, the seven 'missing' LCPs were closing resolutely on the French shore determined to put in their attack.

The surviving LCPs were split into two parties, both oblivious to the others existence. Six of the craft were accompanied by ML346, commanded by Lieutenant Alexander Fear, and continued heading for Yellow I Beach, albeit 25 minutes behind schedule, for the sea fight had caused considerable delay. The other lone survivor, LCP15, commanded by Lieutenant Henry Buckee, carried a party of 20 Commandos led by Captain Peter Young. It was heading for Yellow II Beach. LCP15 had been on the starboard side of the flotilla and had veered away from the action that was taking place on the port beam. Once clear of the sea battle Young and Buckee held a conference and both decided to carry out their attack orders. At 0445hrs, five minutes ahead of schedule and smack on target, Buckee landed Capt Young and his men on Yellow II Beach.

The landing was unopposed and Capt Young, two officers and 17 men disembarked to make their attack on Goebbels Battery. Armed with just one Bren gun, six Thompson sub-machine guns, ten rifles and two mortars, the small band moved up the beach to silence the heavily defended gun battery. The first obstacle they encountered was the barbed wire entanglement blocking the gully that was their exit from the beach. Without wire cutters or Bangalore torpedoes to breach the wire, the Commandos had to haul themselves over it by climbing up the face of the cliff using the supports that were holding barbed wire as footholds and the wire itself for hand holds. After 20 minutes of stiff climbing they reached the top, their hands ripped by the tangled wire and uniforms torn to shreds by the barbs, but they did have the satisfaction of seeing the LCPs of Capt Wills' group arriving on Yellow I Beach and they knew they were not alone.

Young led his Commandos inland in a wide circular movement, which brought them undetected to the rear of Berneval-le-Grand. Their progress through the village itself up to the church was witnessed by only a few of the local population. A few hundred yards away the great guns of the battery had seen the British ships closing on Dieppe and began to open fire. As Young and his men reached the church they were spotted by a German machine-gun. Young had planned to fire down onto the battery from the church tower, but this now proved impossible. The captain decided that he would close on the battery through the nearby orchards, but his group came under fire again. It was clear that the German defences were alert and much too strong for a direct attack, so he withdrew his men into a cornfield to the left and settled them down to harass the enemy gun layers with small arms fire, whilst they waited for the group from Yellow I beach to attack the battery from the other flank.

Five of the craft carrying the other party of 3 Commando and a handful of US Rangers, just 120 men in total, landed on Yellow I Beach at 0515hrs, the sixth boat came in a short while later. By then it was daylight and the German defenders were fully alert. The enemy opened up on the craft just as they came ashore and many men were killed as they clambered out. Most of them, however, made the dash for the shelter of the cliffs where they regrouped and set about tackling the wire blocking the exit. Again the Commandos found they had no Bangalore torpedoes or scaling ladders in their boats, so had to carve a way up the gully through the barbed wire, cutting it by hand as they went. ML346 just offshore supported the move and swept the top of the cliffs with its fire, but a lone German machine-gun continued to give persistent trouble to those braving the exit from the beach. Captain Wills grouped a party of men on the cliff top intending to make a move towards the battery, but first he had to deal with the troublesome machine-gun. He took some Commandos and moved to the left to try to get behind the enemy gun was but hit in the neck and had to retire back to the beach. A little later Capt Osmond led a party across the cliff top and got into the village of Petit Berneval making for the battery. They were almost immediately halted by enemy infantry.

Over on the other side of the battery, Capt Peter Young's group were peppering the enemy gun positions with small arms. The Commandos had little cover in the open cornfields and they felt very exposed. Young settled his men down by informing them that nine feet of standing corn would stop a bullet, so they had nothing to fear! The enemy seemed reluctant to come out of their defences

Troops from 3 Commando land back in Newhaven after their trip to Dieppe. These men all have their full kit and so are probably from those LCPs that abandoned the landings after the fight with the German convoy. (Imperial War Museum, H22588)

to attack the Commando so the harassing fire continued. In desperation, one of the great 150mm guns was turned round and trained on the Commandos, but when it opened fire the shell passed noisily overhead, the gun unable to depress enough to hit a target at such close range. It soon became clear to Young that the dwindling ammunition and the absence of any news from the other party meant that the operation had been unsuccessful. He had succeeded in diverting the battery's attention for a considerable while, but it eventually began to thunder out its fire once again at the warships at sea. There was nothing left now but for the commandos to withdraw. Heading straight for the beach they fired a flare to call the faithful Lt Buckee and his LCP15 back into the landing area to embark them for England.

At about 0530hrs the general alarm was given that landings were taking place all along the coast and German 302nd Division's HQ was quick to react. Major von Blücher, Commander 302nd Anti-tank Battalion, was told to organise an attack against the commandos at Berneval. The major assembled an infantry squadron mounted on bicycles, the 3rd Company of 570th Infantry Regiment and a company of divisional engineers and rushed them to the area. This group, known as 'Blücher Force', arrived to meet both of the parties from Yellow I Beach just as they were trying to move inland. The commandos were quickly pushed back to the beach and tried to get away, but all of the landing craft had already withdrawn under heavy fire or had been sunk. The Commando had no choice but to give up. Of the 120 men that had landed, 37 had been killed, 81 surrendered, most of them wounded; just one man escaped by swimming out to a passing ship. Among the dead was Lieutenant Edward Loustalot, one of the US Rangers accompanying 3 Commando. Loustalot was the first American soldier to be killed in Europe in World War II.

ORANGE BEACH

Whilst 3 Commando was closing on Yellow Beach to begin its attack, the men of 4 Commando had started their run in to Orange Beach from which they would launch their assault on Hess Battery. LtCol The Lord Lovat's men had been transferred from the *Prince Albert* into the seven assault landing craft (LCA) that would take them to the shore. These craft were larger than the LCPs that had carried 3 Commando across the Channel. Each was 41ft long and capable of carrying 40 fully laden troops. At 0350hrs the men of 4 Commando could see the gun fire and flares that lit up the sky away to the east as Commander Wyburd clashed with the German convoy, but Lovat's men continued their run towards the shore thankful they had remained undetected.

At 0430hrs, 20 minutes before they were due to land, the seven craft split into two groups. The larger group of four craft commanded by Lord Lovat swung away to the right to land on Orange II Beach, whilst the remaining three LCAs commanded by Maj Mills-Roberts headed for Orange I Beach. 4 Commando had planned to attack the German battery from two sides. Lord Lovat and his group of 164 men would land at Quiberville (Orange II). They would then advance up the valley of the River Saâne for just over a mile and swing to the left to close on the German battery from the rear. Two miles to the east, Mills-Roberts and 87 men would land at Vasterival (Orange I) and advance directly towards the battery 1,100 yards inland. They would then wait in a wood overlooking the site for Lovat to arrive behind the German guns. The battery was surrounded by a double belt of barbed wire and defended with numerous machine-guns. Overlooking the perimeter was a flak tower containing two 20mm cannons. At 0615hrs Mills-Roberts' men would open fire on the enemy post and occupy its defenders. At 0627hrs Spitfires from the RAF would arrive over the battery and strafe the guns. At 0630hrs Lovat would fire three white Very lights and launch his attack on the battery from the rear covered by a smoke screen laid by Mills-Roberts. Mission accomplished, the Commando would withdraw back to Orange I and embark for home.

Lieutenant-Colonel The Lord Lovat's four landing craft approached Orange II Beach at 0453hrs and were spotted by the enemy just before they arrived on Quiberville beach. A star shell was fired bathing the Commando's run in to the shore in a stark white light. Machine-gun fire from two pillboxes raked the boats but some protection was found by the Commandos inside behind the steel walls of the craft. Once the boats had landed, each of Lovat's men ran straight out and up the beach. Along the top of the seawall was a huge barricade of barbed wire. This obstacle only momentarily stopped the group, for Lovat had already decided on laying a human carpet across the wire, made up of volunteers wearing leather jerkins. These men flung themselves on the wire and others scrambled over them laying heavy coconut matting as they climbed. Some of the men laying the matting were shot, but others quickly took their places. In this

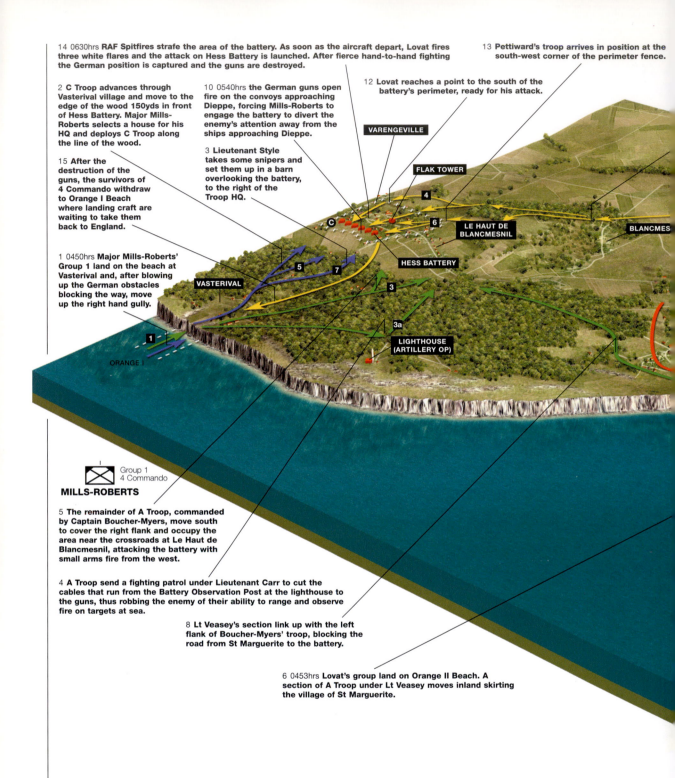

14 0630hrs RAF Spitfires strafe the area of the battery. As soon as the aircraft depart, Lovat fires three white flares and the attack on Hess Battery is launched. After fierce hand-to-hand fighting the German position is captured and the guns are destroyed.

13 Pettiward's troop arrives in position at the south-west corner of the perimeter fence.

2 C Troop advances through Vasterival village and move to the edge of the wood 150yds in front of Hess Battery. Major Mills-Roberts selects a house for his HQ and deploys C Troop along the line of the wood.

10 0540hrs the German guns open fire on the convoys approaching Dieppe, forcing Mills-Roberts to engage the battery to divert the enemy's attention away from the ships approaching Dieppe.

12 Lovat reaches a point to the south of the battery's perimeter, ready for his attack.

VARENGEVILLE

3 Lieutenant Style takes some snipers and set them up in a barn overlooking the battery, to the right of the Troop HQ.

FLAK TOWER

15 After the destruction of the guns, the survivors of 4 Commando withdraw to Orange I Beach where landing craft are waiting to take them back to England.

LE HAUT DE BLANCMESNIL

BLANCMES

C

HESS BATTERY

1 0450hrs Major Mills-Roberts' Group 1 land on the beach at Vasterival and, after blowing up the German obstacles blocking the way, move up the right hand gully.

VASTERIVAL

5 7

3

3a

LIGHTHOUSE (ARTILLERY OP)

1

ORANGE I

Group 1
4 Commando

MILLS-ROBERTS

5 The remainder of A Troop, commanded by Captain Boucher-Myers, move south to cover the right flank and occupy the area near the crossroads at Le Haut de Blancmesnil, attacking the battery with small arms fire from the west.

4 A Troop send a fighting patrol under Lieutenant Carr to cut the cables that run from the Battery Observation Post at the lighthouse to the guns, thus robbing the enemy of their ability to range and observe fire on targets at sea.

8 Lt Veasey's section link up with the left flank of Boucher-Myers' troop, blocking the road from St Marguerite to the battery.

6 0453hrs Lovat's group land on Orange II Beach. A section of A Troop under Lt Veasey moves inland skirting the village of St Marguerite.

4 COMMANDO'S DESTRUCTION OF HESS BATTERY.

19 August 1942, 0450–0900hrs, viewed from the north-west showing the attack on, and destruction of, Hess Battery at Varengeville by Lord Lovat's No. 4 Commando. This is the only significant success of the entire Dieppe operation.

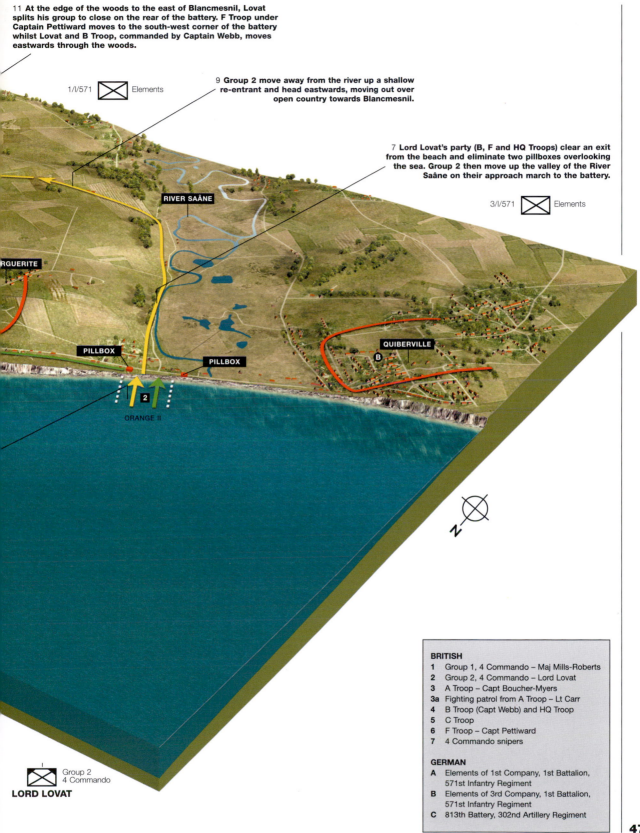

11 At the edge of the woods to the east of Blancmesnil, Lovat splits his group to close on the rear of the battery. F Troop under Captain Pettiward moves to the south-west corner of the battery whilst Lovat and B Troop, commanded by Captain Webb, moves eastwards through the woods.

1/I/571 ⊠ Elements

9 Group 2 move away from the river up a shallow re-entrant and head eastwards, moving out over open country towards Blancmesnil.

7 Lord Lovat's party (B, F and HQ Troops) clear an exit from the beach and eliminate two pillboxes overlooking the sea. Group 2 then move up the valley of the River Saâne on their approach march to the battery.

3/I/571 ⊠ Elements

RIVER SAÂNE

RGUERITE

PILLBOX

PILLBOX

QUIBERVILLE

B

2

ORANGE II

N

⊠ Group 2
4 Commando
LORD LOVAT

BRITISH
1   Group 1, 4 Commando – Maj Mills-Roberts
2   Group 2, 4 Commando – Lord Lovat
3   A Troop – Capt Boucher-Myers
3a Fighting patrol from A Troop – Lt Carr
4   B Troop (Capt Webb) and HQ Troop
5   C Troop
6   F Troop – Capt Pettiward
7   4 Commando snipers

GERMAN
A   Elements of 1st Company, 1st Battalion,
    571st Infantry Regiment
B   Elements of 3rd Company, 1st Battalion,
    571st Infantry Regiment
C   813th Battery, 302nd Artillery Regiment

An assault landing craft on Orange I Beach at Vasterival. The picture was taken during the landing made by Mills-Roberts' party from 4 Commando. To the right is the steep gully through the cliffs up which the commandos had to make their way. In the background, the coast sweeps round to Green Beach, with Dieppe beyond. (Imperial War Museum, HU1833)

way the troops quickly crossed the entanglement and dropped onto the roadway behind the beach. Once off the shoreline, Lieutenant Vesey led a section from A Troop against the two pillboxes, killing the occupants inside with grenades. He then moved off to the east skirting St Marguerite and advanced towards the crossroads beyond, ready to set up a roadblock protecting the Commando from any enemy advancing from the village.

As the landing craft withdrew to wait off shore near Orange I Beach, Lovat led the remainder of his men, from B, F and HQ Troops, on their approach towards the battery. They moved up the right bank of the River Saâne and after about a mile turned east, heading for a small wood to the west of the battery where they would form up for the attack. The time was around 0530hrs and it was broad daylight.

Two miles away, at 0450hrs Mills-Roberts had led his group into Orange I Beach at Vasterival almost under the flashing beam of the lighthouse at d'Ailly. The three craft carrying the commandos landed on the shingle beach completely unobserved by the enemy. There were two exits from the beach, each up a steep gully. Lieutenant Style quickly moved off to examine the one on the left, whilst Mills-Roberts approached the one on the right. At first sight, both looked to be impassable, completely closed off with barbed wire entanglements. The left-hand gully was also blocked by fallen rubble from the cliffs, however, and Mills-Roberts decided that the right-hand gully would be the best option. Bangalore torpedoes were brought forward and a gap was blown through which the men of C Troop scrambled, keeping to the sides of the gully fearing the path to the beach had been mined.

At the top of the cliffs the main body of C Troop moved inland towards the German battery. Lieutenant Carr took a fighting patrol towards the lighthouse and cut the cables leading to it, severing communications between the battery's fire observation post and the guns. Carr and his men then moved inland to the west of the battery to wait. Behind C Troop came A Troop commanded by Captain Boucher-Myers. Its task was to hold the crossroads to the east of St Marguerite and provide right flank protection.

Hess Battery, the rest of the site is now farmland. The bunker now houses a memorial to 4 Commando and those men killed during the raid. (Ken Ford)

By 0540hrs Mills-Roberts and his group had established themselves in a wood close to the battery and had set up posts overlooking the German guns. Almost unbelievably, their approach and consolidation had remained undetected by the enemy. The major now had 35 minutes to wait before, as planned, his group was to open fire. Events, however, overtook him for at that moment the guns opened fire with a booming roar. The ships of the Canadian convoys had been spotted and the guns of Hess Battery were engaging them. This development forced Mills-Roberts' hand. He could not sit idly by whilst the guns did damage to the main operation; he gave the order for his men to fire on the enemy.

Commando officers LtCol The Lord Lovat, Capt Gordon Webb and Capt Boucher-Myers consult with each other after the raid. 4 Commando's casualties during the operation against Hess Battery were 16 killed, 20 wounded and 7 men captured. The complete destruction of the German guns was the one operational success of the raid. (National Archives of Canada, PA-183766)

THE DESTRUCTION OF HESS BATTERY (pages 50–51)

Troop Sergeant-Major Jimmy Dunning (1) directs the fire of his mortar team into the German coastal battery containing six 150mm guns. Privates Dale (2) and Horne (3) have already fired two bombs and Dunning is correcting the aim. Before the third round can be fired the second bomb has plunged into stacked ammunition igniting some cordite and the whole battery erupts in a great fireball (4). The resulting conflagration spreads through the compound and silences the battery for the remainder of the raid. Dunning and his team had set up their mortar on the edge of the small wood adjacent to the enemy position. Major Mills Roberts and his men had arrived completely undetected at 0545hrs, hoping to hold their fire until just before Lord Lovat made his attack on the other side of the battery at 0630hrs. When the German guns engaged the ships carrying the Canadians into Dieppe, however, they had little choice but to open fire. Mills Roberts then ordered his commandos to harass the enemy garrison with their small arms to stop the guns firing. In reply, the Germans in the flak tower (5) sprayed the edge of the woods with their anti-aircraft cannon, causing some casualties. Fortunately, the lucky shot from Sergeant-Major Dunning's mortar diverted attention away from the commandos. Jimmy Dunning was a veteran of the earlier raids including that carried out by 4 Commando against

Vaagsö in December 1941. After Dieppe he became an instructor at the Commando Training Centre at Achnacarry and later served in Palestine, Korea and took part in the invasion of Suez in 1956. Lord Lovat had little use for the British steel helmet and insisted that his men went into action wearing 'cap comforters' (6). He commented that a steel helmet, 'Slows down a man like a grand piano, for it fetters him at his point of balance'. He thought that what was good for trench warfare in 1915 was quite unsuitable for mobile troops. On their feet, the commandos wore Boots SV (7). These were leather boots with cleated rubber soles – known to the public as 'commando' soles – designed specifically for use on special assignments. The rubber compound gave a good grip when climbing or traversing wet rocks. Each man was ordered to wear a life jacket during the raid (8). They were universally known as a 'Mae West,' and were named after the popular and voluptuous film star. The 2in. mortar (9) used by the commandos was the British Army's standard infantry platoon support weapon. It weighed 4.1lbs (3.3kg), had a maximum range of 500yds (450m) and fired a 2.2lb (1kg) HE bomb which, on hard ground, had a burst radius of around 165yds (150m). The mortar, which also fired smoke, illumination rounds and signal flares, remained in British service until the early 1980s. (Howard Gerrard)

The first shots caused some puzzlement to the gun crews as men began falling dead around the battery from some unseen cause. The soldiers in the flak tower could see the muzzle flashes of the British Bren guns and rifles, however, and shells from the light cannon began spraying the edge of the wood. The Commandos peppered the flak tower with anti-tank rifle fire and the cannon soon fell quiet. Commando snipers continued to pick off individuals as the German crews tried to concentrate on serving the guns. One of the snipers was Corporal Franklin Koons of the US Rangers. He was credited as being the first American to kill a German soldier in World War II.

Troop Sergeant-Major Jimmy Dunning set up his 2in. mortar close to the edge of the woods and his two-man team of Privates Dale and Horne now opened fire on the battery. The first bomb they fired fell short. Dunning shouted a correction and they fired again. The second bomb was spot on and descended into a pile of cordite stacked by one of the guns. There was an immense explosion as the ammunition ignited, followed by screams and chaos as raging fires broke out all over the battery. All of the guns fell silent; the battery did not fire another shot.

A mile away Lovat and his men were cheered by the explosion. When they reached the woods to the rear of the battery the group split up prior to the assault on the guns. F Troop under Capt Pettiward moved through the woods to the south-west corner of the battery, whilst Lovat and B Troop, commanded by Capt Gordon Webb, closed on the south-facing rear of the defended gun site, fighting with enemy snipers on the way. Capt Pettiward was killed near the exit of the wood and, although wounded in the hand, Capt Pat Porteous took over F Troop. Once in position Lovat and his men waited for the moment to launch the attack. Over to the west of the lodgement German reinforcements coming from St Marguerite were ambushed by A Troop and eliminated.

Right on time at around 0630hrs RAF Spitfires screamed low over the battery firing cannons and machine guns at the disorganised German defenders. Immediately after the air strike, three Very lights were fired and Lovat's 4 Commando rushed the battery. F Troop attacked the guns whilst B Troop cleared the buildings. One of the first into the battery was Capt Pat Porteous who fell across one of the guns shot through the thigh. He picked himself up and continued to lead the charge, killing Germans as he went. He was shot again. He continued until the guns were taken and then collapsed through loss of blood. For his gallantry that day he was awarded the Victoria Cross. Right across the battery the Commandos ran amongst the enemy shooting, grenading and bayoneting every German they found. The fighting was over quickly and F Troop then set demolition charges around each of the guns to blow the barrels and breach blocks. Other charges were placed in underground ammunition dumps. The dead and wounded Commandos were all brought together and a Union Jack was spread in front of them as a signal to the RAF that the battery had fallen. Once the work was done, the charges were blown and Lovat and his men retired down the path to Orange I Beach to the waiting landing craft. The withdrawal was orderly and well controlled, the enemy never being allowed to approach too close to the rearguard. All the men that were able to make it to the boats were evacuated. Lovat's men had carried out a text-book Commando operation to perfection.

Unteroffizier Leo Marsiniak is landed at Newhaven as a prisoner, brought back from the gun battery at Varengeville by 4 Commando. (Imperial War Museum, H22597)

Capt Gordon Webb with his arm in a sling talks to Lt Len Coulson after they had returned to Newhaven. Capt Webb was wounded by a mortar fragment early in the morning and continued to lead his men throughout the battle even though his right arm was rendered useless. (Canada Dept of National Defence/National Archives of Canada, PA-113250)

BLUE BEACH

Blue Beach was just a mile to the east of Dieppe at Puys, separated from the port by the towering chalk cliffs of the eastern headland. The beach was short and narrow, just 275yds long, backed by a 10ft-high sea wall. The village of Puys wound inland from the sea, its houses clinging to the sides of a steep gully. Covering the sea wall and the narrow exit inland were several German pillboxes, sited to cover the entire beach with interlocking fields of fire. On top of the sea wall was a formidable barrier of multiple layers of barbed wire. Success depended on surprise and getting off the beach as quickly as possible. Neither were to be achieved.

The Royal Regiment of Canada was to land on Blue Beach, move through Puys, swing to the right and advance onto the eastern headland overlooking Dieppe to meet up with troops from the Essex Scottish, who were to land on Red Beach close to the port entrance. The Royals were also to capture the German field gun battery codenamed 'Rommel' and eliminate the anti-aircraft site behind Puys. Commanding the Royal Regiment was LtCol Douglas Cato. He planned to land with four companies of his battalion, a total of 554 men, in three waves. The first wave, the main assault, contained three companies; the second wave ten minutes later consisted of one company and Battalion HQ, whilst the third wave comprised a special force from other units. Included in this number were some men from the Royal Canadian Artillery who were to take over the guns of Rommel Battery and turn them on the enemy. Also included was a company of the Black Watch of Canada to cover the eastern flank of the lodgement whilst the Royals advanced on Dieppe. One of the key factors to achieving success in the landings on Blue and Green Beaches was the element of surprise. In view of this, there was to be no prior bombardment of the beach defences by warships.

After the craft carrying the Royal Regiment had been lowered from the landing ships, there was some delay in forming up correctly and starting out for the shore. Timing at this point was crucial to the operation. When these craft finally approached Blue Beach at 0506hrs they were 16 minutes late and it was much lighter than had been intended. The delay also meant that actions already taking place elsewhere had alerted the Germans in the pillboxes and manning machine-guns in houses overlooking the beach who were ready for the Canadians.

Enemy fire hit the landing craft from the moment they came into range. As the small boats grounded on the beach and dropped their ramps, they were struck by a torrent of machine-gun fire that devastated the Canadian troops inside. Without leaving the small boats countless men were mown down where they stood. Men cowered to the open sides as though they were sheltering from the rain, but there was little cover to be had in the open-fronted craft. The more determined of the Royals braved the whirlwind of bullets and ran pell-mell for the sea wall, hugging its towering stone sides to escape the German fusillade. Pillboxes on the cliffs to the left looked down along almost the entire line of the wall, allowing the German troops inside to pick off individuals one by one.

Within just seconds order was completely lost. The assault wave of the battalion had become a disorganised mass of individuals each seeking some shelter from the hail of fire. Every time some effort was made to surmount the wall and blow the wire, the men attempting the feat were destroyed by machine-guns. For 20 minutes officers tried to regroup the men and find a way off the beach. Then the second wave arrived. It too received the full weight of the enemy fire from close range, decimating the men in the landing craft and those that braved the open beach. The whole attack was failing badly.

Great acts of heroism took place on Blue Beach that morning. A breach was made in the wire and LtCol Cato and a few men got off the beach into houses on the right, but their progress inland was slow and costly. This small party made it to the top of the cliff but no others were able to join it, the gap in the wire having been effectively closed by interdictory fire. Then came the third wave of the Black Watch of Canada onto Blue Beach. Their craft veered to the right when they saw the devastation ahead of them and they landed on the shingle under the cliffs. It was a pointless exercise, for the exposed men could do nothing but shelter beneath the overhanging cliff away from enemy fire. Any attempt to move out into the open to join with the others or fight towards an exit brought certain death.

Few of the landing craft that made it onto Blue Beach left unscathed. None of the exposed boats could survive there under the devastating enemy fire; the only chance was to withdraw. There was no question of waiting for the Royals to abandon or complete their mission, no sooner had the landing craft shed their loads, than they reversed off the shingle and tried to put out to sea. Many of them got no further out than the shallows before they were knocked out, sunk or set on fire. The attack had become a bloody shambles and the Royal Regiment was left to its fate.

GREEN BEACH

To the right of Dieppe, on the other side of the western headland, the white cliffs dip down to the seaside village of Pourville. This was the location of Green Beach, the target for the South Saskatchewan Regiment.

This beach was longer than that at Puys, but still dominated by high ground on both sides. The dip in the cliffs had been carved out by the River Scie, which reached the sea on the left (east) side of the beach. The river had been dammed by the Germans just behind the shore to form a large lake and waterlogged ground that acted as an anti-tank barrier. Behind the beach was a low sea wall topped by wire. At the rear of this was a lateral road that climbed eastwards over the cliffs towards Dieppe. Halfway up the cliffs was a radar station, the capture of which was one of the prime objectives of the raid. The enemy had not turned the low-lying village of Pourville into a strongpoint, but had built positions on the cliffs to the east inside the great defensive perimeter that circled Dieppe. These pillboxes were scattered across hills overlooking the village, the anchor of the defense being Quatre Vents Farm, a range of buildings that had a commanding view of the whole valley. The farm had been turned into a veritable fortress.

The South Saskatchewans were to land on Green Beach astride the mouth of the River Scie. The right-hand group, comprising B and C Companies, would move off the beach and into Pourville, then clear the cliffs to the west. The left-hand group, A and D Companies, would clear the beach to the east, capture the radar station and attack Quatre Vents Farm, before overrunning the western headland, overlooking Dieppe, from the rear. Landing behind the Saskatchewans would be the Queen's Own Cameron Highlanders. Their task was to advance inland along the eastern bank of the River Scie to meet up with tanks coming from Dieppe and capture the aerodrome at St Aubin. Next they would clear the 'Hitler' Battery and attack the supposed German divisional HQ at Arques-la-Bataille.

The assault across Green Beach took place exactly on time with the South Saskatchewans coming ashore at 0450hrs. They did not, however, land astride the mouth of the River Scie as planned: missing their landfall in the poor light they landed to the west of the river. This did not present a problem for the two companies who were to clear the village and attack the west cliff, but the men who were to take the eastern headland now had to first get through the village, then cross the exposed bridge over the river before they could get onto the high ground. This delay proved fatal as the initial advantage of surprise was lost and the enemy had time to react and deploy.

A and D Companies cleared the village and occupied all their objectives, including the large white house on the west cliff, which proved to be some kind of German officers' quarters. They also killed and captured a great many of the enemy in the process. The other two companies fared less well for as they worked eastwards and tried to cross the river bridge, the enemy pillboxes on the high ground facing them swept the crossing place with accurate fire. The German positions completely dominated the bridge and the eastern side of the village. Attempts were made to cross the river, but each failed with great loss of life. The bridge became carpeted with Canadian dead and the advance stalled.

It took an act of individual bravery to restore the attack's momentum. Lieutenant-Colonel Charles Merritt, commander of the South Saskatchewans, came forward to rally his men. With great gallantry he walked out onto the bridge and urged the troops to do the same. A handful of men summoned the courage required to make the dash across and a few others subsequently joined them. Back and forth, the colonel crossed and re-crossed the bridge escorting new groups as he went, calling, 'See, there is no danger here!' Then he joined his men on the far side and led a series of attacks on the enemy's concrete emplacements. Wherever the action was hottest, there was Colonel Merritt. For his great valour that day LtCol Charles Merritt was awarded the Victoria Cross.

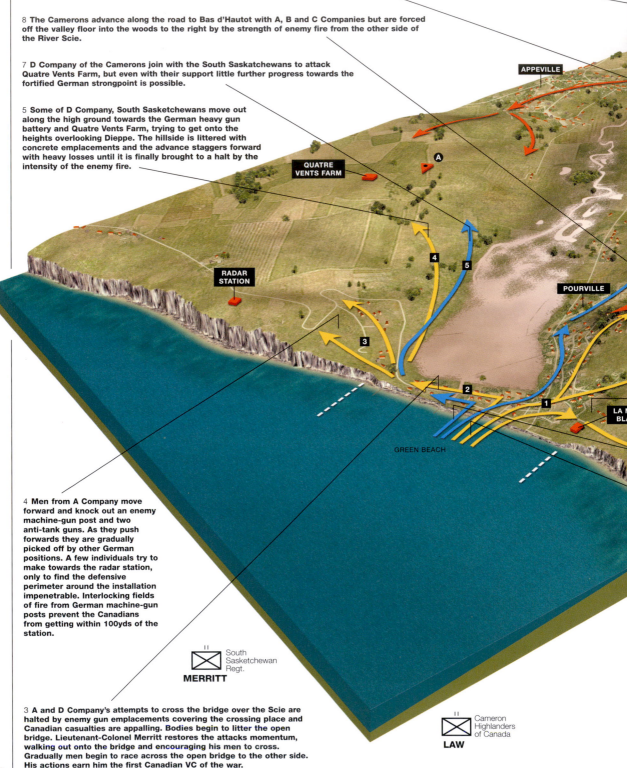

11 0845hrs Whilst A Company secures the high ground on the right, B and C Companies move to seize the bridge over the Scie at Petit Appeville. The Camerons, however, are beaten to the bridge by enemy troops from 1st Battalion, 571st Regiment. The bridge is covered by two 75mm guns and, with no sign of any Canadian tanks coming up from Dieppe, Major Law realises that any further advance inland is impossible. He orders a withdrawal to the beaches.

10 571st Regiment's Anti-Tank Company and the Infantry Gun Platoon are sent north to support the area around Quatre Vents Farm.

8 The Camerons advance along the road to Bas d'Hautot with A, B and C Companies but are forced off the valley floor into the woods to the right by the strength of enemy fire from the other side of the River Scie.

7 D Company of the Camerons join with the South Saskatchewans to attack Quatre Vents Farm, but even with their support little further progress towards the fortified German strongpoint is possible.

5 Some of D Company, South Sasketchewans move out along the high ground towards the German heavy gun battery and Quatre Vents Farm, trying to get onto the heights overlooking Dieppe. The hillside is littered with concrete emplacements and the advance staggers forward with heavy losses until it is finally brought to a halt by the intensity of the enemy fire.

QUATRE VENTS FARM

APPEVILLE

RADAR STATION

POURVILLE

LA MA BLAN

GREEN BEACH

4 Men from A Company move forward and knock out an enemy machine-gun post and two anti-tank guns. As they push forwards they are gradually picked off by other German positions. A few individuals try to make towards the radar station, only to find the defensive perimeter around the installation impenetrable. Interlocking fields of fire from German machine-gun posts prevent the Canadians from getting within 100yds of the station.

South
Sasketchewan
Regt.

MERRITT

Cameron
Highlanders
of Canada

LAW

3 A and D Company's attempts to cross the bridge over the Scie are halted by enemy gun emplacements covering the crossing place and Canadian casualties are appalling. Bodies begin to litter the open bridge. Lieutenant-Colonel Merritt restores the attacks momentum, walking out onto the bridge and encouraging his men to cross. Gradually men begin to race across the open bridge to the other side. His actions earn him the first Canadian VC of the war.

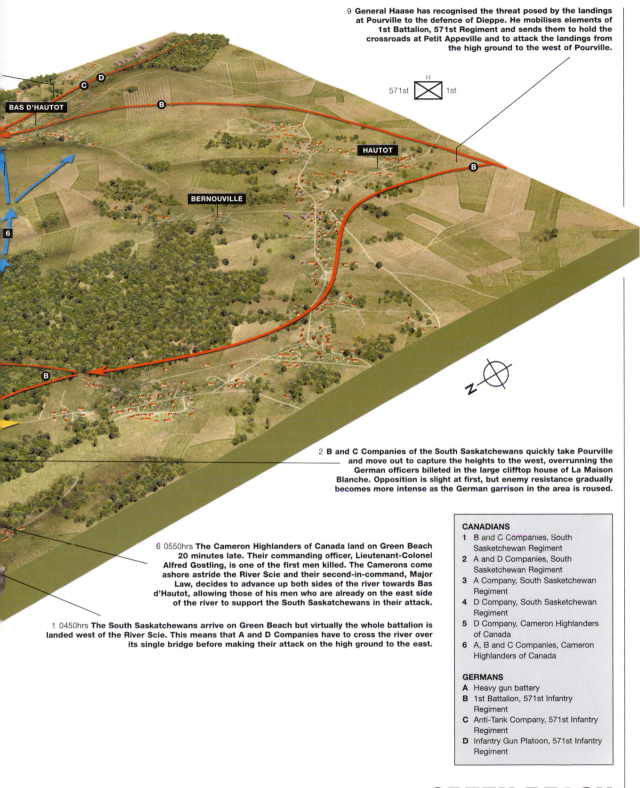

9 General Haase has recognised the threat posed by the landings at Pourville to the defence of Dieppe. He mobilises elements of 1st Battalion, 571st Regiment and sends them to hold the crossroads at Petit Appeville and to attack the landings from the high ground to the west of Pourville.

571st 1st

BAS D'HAUTOT

HAUTOT

BERNOUVILLE

2 B and C Companies of the South Saskatchewans quickly take Pourville and move out to capture the heights to the west, overrunning the German officers billeted in the large clifftop house of La Maison Blanche. Opposition is slight at first, but enemy resistance gradually becomes more intense as the German garrison in the area is roused.

6 0550hrs The Cameron Highlanders of Canada land on Green Beach 20 minutes late. Their commanding officer, Lieutenant-Colonel Alfred Gostling, is one of the first men killed. The Camerons come ashore astride the River Scie and their second-in-command, Major Law, decides to advance up both sides of the river towards Bas d'Hautot, allowing those of his men who are already on the east side of the river to support the South Saskatchewans in their attack.

1 0450hrs The South Saskatchewans arrive on Green Beach but virtually the whole battalion is landed west of the River Scie. This means that A and D Companies have to cross the river over its single bridge before making their attack on the high ground to the east.

CANADIANS
1 B and C Companies, South Sasketchewan Regiment
2 A and D Companies, South Sasketchewan Regiment
3 A Company, South Sasketchewan Regiment
4 D Company, South Sasketchewan Regiment
5 D Company, Cameron Highlanders of Canada
6 A, B and C Companies, Cameron Highlanders of Canada

GERMANS
A Heavy gun battery
B 1st Battalion, 571st Infantry Regiment
C Anti-Tank Company, 571st Infantry Regiment
D Infantry Gun Platoon, 571st Infantry Regiment

GREEN BEACH
19 August 1942, 0455–0845hrs, viewed from the north-west showing the South Sasketchewans' and Camerons' abortive attacks.

Several of the enemy positions on the heights were taken, but despite great effort and astounding courage the troops could not clear the area. Progress completely stalled as each man was forced to seek cover from withering enemy fire. All was not lost, however, as behind them help was arriving in the shape of the Cameron Highlanders as they stormed onto Green Beach, pipes playing.

The Camerons arrived 30 minutes late, at 0550hrs. The delay was intentional as their commander did not believe that the Saskatchewans could clear the beach and the village in the allowed 30 minutes, so he had put back his battalion's arrival. When they did land, the first man to be killed as the landing craft ran up the shingle was the CO himself, LtCol Alfred Gostling. Again mistakes were made and most of the assault craft arrived in the wrong place west of the river, whereas the bulk of the men should have been set down to the east of the river ready to advance up the right bank of the valley. Major Tony Law took command of the battalion and decided to alter the plan and move inland up the western side of the Scie. Those Camerons that had already arrived on the eastern side were told to join with the Saskatchewans and help clear the high ground.

Major Law's group moved off inland along the road towards Bas d'Hautot and Petit Appeville. They were harassed all the way by the enemy in Quatre Vents Farm across the river. To escape the worst of this fire, Law took his men up onto the high ground to his right and advanced under cover of trees to a point above Bas d'Hautot. From here they could look down on their first objective, the bridge across the River Scie at Petit Appeville. To Major Law's dismay he saw that the enemy already held the bridge in some force. The landings at Pourville had alerted 571st Regiment, and the divisional commander, GenLt Haase, knew that any attempt to close on Dieppe from inland would have to pass over the bridge at Petit Appeville. He sent a bicycle platoon from the Regiment's I Battalion at Ouville to hold the bridge and ordered an anti-tank company and an infantry gun platoon forward to join it. By the time Maj Law arrived with his party of Camerons the bridge was already protected by light artillery and infantry. With nothing more than the weapons they were carrying, the Commandos could not mount an attack against the bridge. Nor could they bypass it for the road from Ouville was now swarming with enemy soldiers.

Back on the eastern cliffs the Saskatchewans and the Camerons managed to close in on the radar station and to the trenches surrounding Quatre Vents Farm, but each time they pressed home their attack they were beaten back by enemy fire. German reinforcements were now arriving on the heights and the position for the Canadians was becoming untenable.

THE MAIN ASSAULT

The main objective of Operation Jubilee was the attack on Dieppe itself and it was here across the town's beach that the bulk of the raiding force was to be committed. The seafront at Dieppe is about a mile long, the shingle beach backed by a low sea wall mostly rising little more than 5ft above the pebbles. In the centre a mechanical excavator was in the process of carving a deep antitank ditch through the pebbles, however. Behind the sea wall, and stretching inland for about 220yds, was an open esplanade of parks and gardens. Beyond this were the buildings of the town, mainly hotels and large houses, along the Boulevard de Verdun. At the right end of the beach, underneath the high western headland, was the town's Casino; a large white building empty since the start of the war and fortified with the addition of two pillboxes alongside facing the shore.

The two headlands at either end of the beach were known to be fortified by the enemy, but the Allied planners had no clear idea of the strength of these fortifications. In fact the Germans had covered the eastern headland with machine gun posts and light weapons, all sited to command the beach. They were skilfully built into caves and embrasures and almost invisible from the sea. The same was true to a lesser extent of the western headland. At the top of the beach was a double row of wire, one on the shingle and one, over 6½ft thick, on top of the sea wall. All the roads leading from the promenade into the town were blocked by 7ft-high concrete walls, 5ft thick and surmounted by barbed wire, effectively sealing off the seafront from the town with a ring of concrete.

The wide expanse of shingle on Red Beach at Dieppe close to the harbour entrance. In the background the eastern headland overlooks the landing place. The face of these sheer chalk cliffs had many machine gun posts built into caves and dug-outs along their length. (Ken Ford)

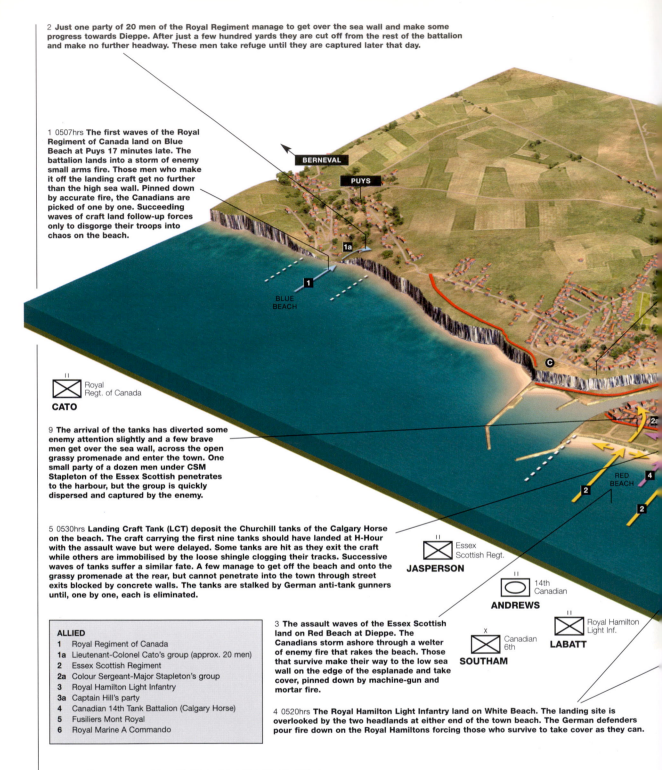

2 Just one party of 20 men of the Royal Regiment manage to get over the sea wall and make some progress towards Dieppe. After just a few hundred yards they are cut off from the rest of the battalion and make no further headway. These men take refuge until they are captured later that day.

1 0507hrs The first waves of the Royal Regiment of Canada land on Blue Beach at Puys 17 minutes late. The battalion lands into a storm of enemy small arms fire. Those men who make it off the landing craft get no further than the high sea wall. Pinned down by accurate fire, the Canadians are picked of one by one. Succeeding waves of craft land follow-up forces only to disgorge their troops into chaos on the beach.

BERNEVAL

PUYS

1a

1

BLUE BEACH

Royal Regt. of Canada
CATO

9 The arrival of the tanks has diverted some enemy attention slightly and a few brave men get over the sea wall, across the open grassy promenade and enter the town. One small party of a dozen men under CSM Stapleton of the Essex Scottish penetrates to the harbour, but the group is quickly dispersed and captured by the enemy.

5 0530hrs Landing Craft Tank (LCT) deposit the Churchill tanks of the Calgary Horse on the beach. The craft carrying the first nine tanks should have landed at H-Hour with the assault wave but were delayed. Some tanks are hit as they exit the craft while others are immobilised by the loose shingle clogging their tracks. Successive waves of tanks suffer a similar fate. A few manage to get off the beach and onto the grassy promenade at the rear, but cannot penetrate into the town through street exits blocked by concrete walls. The tanks are stalked by German anti-tank gunners until, one by one, each is eliminated.

c

RED BEACH

2

2

4

2

Essex Scottish Regt.
JASPERSON

14th Canadian
ANDREWS

3 The assault waves of the Essex Scottish land on Red Beach at Dieppe. The Canadians storm ashore through a welter of enemy fire that rakes the beach. Those that survive make their way to the low sea wall on the edge of the esplanade and take cover, pinned down by machine-gun and mortar fire.

Canadian 6th
SOUTHAM

Royal Hamilton Light Inf.
LABATT

4 0520hrs The Royal Hamilton Light Infantry land on White Beach. The landing site is overlooked by the two headlands at either end of the town beach. The German defenders pour fire down on the Royal Hamiltons forcing those who survive to take cover as they can.

ALLIED	
1	Royal Regiment of Canada
1a	Lieutenant-Colonel Cato's group (approx. 20 men)
2	Essex Scottish Regiment
2a	Colour Sergeant-Major Stapleton's group
3	Royal Hamilton Light Infantry
3a	Captain Hill's party
4	Canadian 14th Tank Battalion (Calgary Horse)
5	Fusiliers Mont Royal
6	Royal Marine A Commando

ASSAULT ON DIEPPE

19 August, 0507–0830hrs, viewed from the north-west showing the disastrous landings on Red and White beaches by Canadian 4th Infantry Brigade. The landings are pinned down on the beaches amid heavy casualties and only a few tanks and a handful of men manage to cross the seawall and promenade as far as the houses and hotels on Boulevard de Verdun.

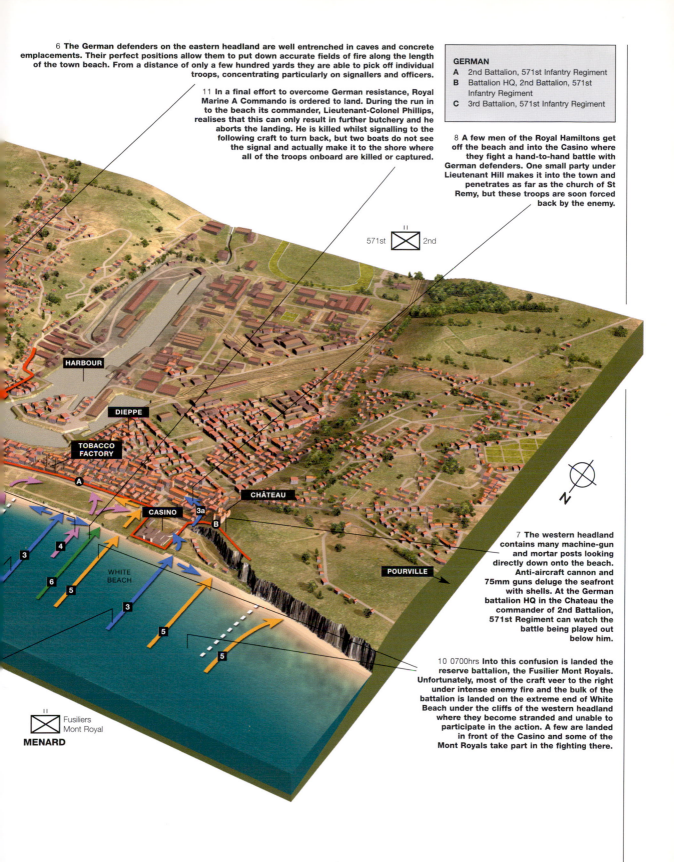

6 The German defenders on the eastern headland are well entrenched in caves and concrete emplacements. Their perfect positions allow them to put down accurate fields of fire along the length of the town beach. From a distance of only a few hundred yards they are able to pick off individual troops, concentrating particularly on signallers and officers.

11 In a final effort to overcome German resistance, Royal Marine A Commando is ordered to land. During the run in to the beach its commander, Lieutenant-Colonel Phillips, realises that this can only result in further butchery and he aborts the landing. He is killed whilst signalling to the following craft to turn back, but two boats do not see the signal and actually make it to the shore where all of the troops onboard are killed or captured.

GERMAN

A 2nd Battalion, 571st Infantry Regiment
B Battalion HQ, 2nd Battalion, 571st Infantry Regiment
C 3rd Battalion, 571st Infantry Regiment

8 A few men of the Royal Hamiltons get off the beach and into the Casino where they fight a hand-to-hand battle with German defenders. One small party under Lieutenant Hill makes it into the town and penetrates as far as the church of St Remy, but these troops are soon forced back by the enemy.

571st ⊠ 2nd

HARBOUR

DIEPPE

TOBACCO FACTORY

A

CASINO

3a

CHÂTEAU

B

POURVILLE

WHITE BEACH

7 The western headland contains many machine-gun and mortar posts looking directly down onto the beach. Anti-aircraft cannon and 75mm guns deluge the seafront with shells. At the German battalion HQ in the Chateau the commander of 2nd Battalion, 571st Regiment can watch the battle being played out below him.

10 0700hrs Into this confusion is landed the reserve battalion, the Fusilier Mont Royals. Unfortunately, most of the craft veer to the right under intense enemy fire and the bulk of the battalion is landed on the extreme end of White Beach under the cliffs of the western headland where they become stranded and unable to participate in the action. A few are landed in front of the Casino and some of the Mont Royals take part in the fighting there.

⊠ Fusiliers Mont Royal

MENARD

These barriers were further fortified with machine-guns. Some even had 75mm and 37mm weapons supporting them.

The beach at Dieppe was divided by the planners into two landing areas: Red Beach on the left close to the harbour mouth and White Beach on the right with its flank alongside the western headland. Red Beach was to be attacked by the Essex Scottish Regiment, White Beach by the Royal Hamilton Light Infantry. The Essex Scottish was to concentrate on capturing the town and harbour and moving onto the eastern headland to meet with the Royals coming from Blue Beach. The Hamilton Light Infantry was ordered to capture the western part of the town, attack the western headland and join up with the Saskatchewans from Green Beach and to seize the heavy Göring Battery behind Dieppe.

Landing eight of its tanks with the assault waves on White Beach and following up with the remainder of its armour in successive waves was the 14th Canadian Tank Battalion (the Calgary Tanks). It was tasked with helping to capture the town and then moving inland to meet with the Cameron Highlanders from Green Beach to attack the airfield at St Aubin and the suspected German divisional HQ at Arques-la-Bataille.

Jubilee called for the flank attacks to go in over Blue and Green Beaches 30 minutes before the landings at Dieppe. In that way both of the headlands overlooking the town would be under attack from the rear when the main attack arrived on the town beach. The early capture of these headlands was therefore vital to the overall plan, for continued enemy possession of the heights would eventually make the main beach untenable. It was also imperative that the assault troops get off the beach away from fire from the headlands as soon as possible. To stay on the shore would invite certain death. However, once the flank attacks were launched it would be obvious to the enemy that further landings would take place in Dieppe itself. Surprise would, therefore, inevitably be lost, so hope of success would rely on effective naval and aerial support and, most importantly, on the speed of execution by the assaulting troops. They had to get off the beach and into the town.

At 0502hrs a few miles off Dieppe the destroyers *Berkeley*, *Bleasdale*, *Garth* and *Albrighton* and the gun boat *Locust* spread out and took up bombarding positions astern of the landing craft taking the Essex Scottish and the Royal Hamilton Light Infantry to the beaches. Ten minutes later the naval vessels opened up on the buildings lining the seafront at Dieppe with their 4in. guns. Three buildings were set on fire then the destroyers switched their attention to the enemy positions on the two headlands. At the same time the RAF attacked the headlands with bombs and cannon fire. As the aircraft climbed away and roared back out over the Channel, a second wave came in and dropped smoke bombs to shroud the heights in an acrid fog. At 0523hrs the assault waves landed on Red and White Beaches, just three minutes late.

The enemy's fire was not heavy at first and the landing craft set down their loads without too much opposition, backing off into open sea without loss. The troops got ashore with few casualties and began making for the first belt of wire across 90yds of open beach. They got through the first entanglement and headed for the next belt of wire on the sea wall. Then things began to go wrong. The enemy, now recovered from the bombardment, had taken up positions overlooking the seafront and opened a heavy fire on the Canadians. The storm of machine-gun bullets

The view across the promenade from near the junction of Red and White Beaches in Dieppe, taken after the raid. German engineers are recovering tanks from the beach, using the Churchill called 'Bert' to tow the disabled 'Chief' over the sea wall. The sea wall did not prove to be a problem for the tanks after they had landed, for some of the Canadian armour were easily able to negotiate their way over it and onto the grassy promenade to the rear. The two chimneys in the background belong to the Tobacco Factory, set on fire during the bombardment. (Bundesarchiv, 101/292/1242/6)

and mortar bombs began inflicting casualties on the troops on the open beach and men instinctively sought shelter behind the sea wall and in dips in the shingle banks. Ahead of them was the thick second belt of barbed wire entanglements with 220yds of open ground beyond that. Each time men tried to breach the wire they were killed. The moment anyone showed their head above the wall they became the target of a sniper. Most of the men hugged the ground digging into the shingle for cover, waiting for some order to appear from the chaos.

Most alarming to the exposed troops was the fire sweeping along the beach from the headlands on their flanks. The German positions were virtually impossible to locate and, shielded as they were from the sea, impervious to the naval gunfire. Whilst German machine-guns and mortars swept the beach, enemy snipers picked off men one by one. The conspicuous radio sets strapped to their backs made signallers obvious targets. Those that tried to take cover from the fire were shot the moment they raised their aerials and tried to transmit to the ships at sea. There were many other important and obvious targets for the snipers. Officers suffered especially badly as they stood up and tried to rally their men. Mortar crews and machine-gunners, engineers and demolition men all became victims, the enemy marksmen drawn to them by their bulky weapons and equipment. Pinned down as they were, it soon became clear to the Canadians that the best way to stay alive on the beach was to play dead.

The troops landing on Red and White Beaches should have had the cover and firepower of tanks to support them from the moment they landed, but none had arrived. The Essex Scottish and the Hamiltons were on the exposed beach for ten minutes before the first LCTs with the vital armour crashed through the surf. Thus in those first crucial minutes, just when it was most vital, the infantry were deprived of valuable covering fire.

The first three LCTs arrived between 0533hrs and 0538hrs with nine Churchill tanks. By then the beach was alive with enemy fire. The heavier German weapons began to concentrate their fire on the LCTs as they approached the shoreline out of the smoke. None of the vessels escaped unscathed. A short time later the second wave of three LCTs arrived to deliver their complement of tanks into the melee and these landing craft also became the targets of German shells.

LCT 145 successfully landed her three tanks, but was repeatedly hit as she withdrew, disabled and sunk offshore. Also sunk after withdrawing from the beach was LCT 126, but not before she had safely landed her tanks. LCT 127 sustained heavy damage after she had completed her mission and most of her crew were killed or wounded, but she did manage to withdraw out to sea and get away. LCT 159 was hit approaching the shore and she came in with her ramp half down; by the time she had offloaded her armour she was completely disabled and could not get off the beach. Also stuck on the shore was LCT 121, disabled by enemy shells. The crew of LCT 163 persevered in no fewer than four attempts to get in to the shore, the first three attempts failed and she lost her helmsman.

The third wave of four LCTs following 30 minutes later received further punishment. LCT 124 landed her tanks and withdrew only to be sunk later. LCT 125 landed just one tank before her master was then ordered by the beachmaster to withdraw. Why LCT 125 was ordered to withdraw is not known. About 45 minutes later LCT 125 returned and was again beached, but all her officers and crew were killed or wounded in the attempt. A second tank managed to get off the craft before one of her injured officers withdrew the boat out to sea where she was taken in tow by HMS *Alresford*. LCT 165 had her steering gear hit on the run in but she beached successfully and landed her tanks. She then managed to get away to sea and was later repaired. Finally, LCT 166 landed her tanks without difficulty and withdrew. In total, 28 out of the 30 tanks allocated to the operation were landed over Red and White Beaches. Of these only two were 'drowned' in deep water.

One of the landing craft tank (LCT 159) that brought the armour of the Calgary Regiment onto the beach. The LCTs were the largest ships to come into shore and their commanding bulk made them tempting targets for enemy artillery. LCT 159 was in the first wave of tank landing craft and was disabled the moment she touched down at around 0530hrs. (National Archives of Canada, C-17292)

The arrival of the tanks on the beach should have enabled the Canadians to break the deadlock. The tanks should have provided sufficient cover and supporting fire to allow the advance into Dieppe town to resume. In reality the tanks found it difficult to gain traction on the loose shingle and large pebbles of the beach. The churning tracks often dug deep trenches in the shingle forcing stones up between the tank's drive wheels and tracks causing them to fail. Those tanks that did manage to cross the treacherous shingle, crash through the wire and over the sea wall had to run the gauntlet of numerous enemy antitank guns. Once onto the open gardens beyond the beach they were less vulnerable to this shelling, but to their bitter disappointment they found they were unable to breach the concrete roadblocks that barred every exit from the seafront. The engineers that should have moved up with the armour to breach the concrete walls were all stuck on the beach or in the crippled and burning LCTs along with their equipment. Some 15 tanks succeeded in making it off the beach but could do little more than roar up and down the promenade in impotent rage, firing at targets of opportunity and receiving a peppering of enemy shells in return. Many of them later returned to the beach in frustration where they served as nothing more than mobile pillboxes until their ammunition ran out.

Courage and determination enabled a few of the Essex Scottish to make it over the sea wall and across the seafront promenade. One party led by Colour Sergeant-Major Stapleton blew a gap in the wire with a Bangalore torpedo and, in the smoke and confusion that accompanied the arrival of the tanks, made it across the promenade and into houses along the Boulevard de Verdun. The sergeant-major gathered his group and led them through to the Quai du Hable overlooking the harbour, but was injured by a sniper and captured. The rest of his party scattered and was driven back by the volume of fire coming from the eastern headland. A further group of eight also pressed on from the beach and attempted to gain the hotels on the far side of the gardens lining the boulevard, but seven fell to German fire in the attempt, leaving just Private Fleming alone surrounded by the enemy.

At the other end of the landings, the Hamiltons on White Beach had a little more success. A number of them got off the beach and knocked out the pillboxes by the side of the Casino. They infiltrated the large white building and had a running battle with the Germans inside, killing and wounding all they found. For a while the Casino was held against repeated attempts by the enemy to recapture it. From its windows Bren gunners were able to give covering fire to others attempting to get off the beach. Lieutenant Tony Hill led a group of about a dozen Hamiltons from the Casino across the Boulevard du Verdun and into the buildings of the town. They tried unsuccessfully to scale one of the tank barriers, but enemy fire forced them to abandon the attempt. Instead they broke through the windows of a seafront building and got out through the back. Snipers tracked their progress, harassing them with interdictory fire. They exchanged shots with German patrols as they edged their way into the town, but the gathering numbers of the enemy forced them back to a cinema. Here Lt Hill was joined by another party of Hamiltons led by Maj Lazier. While the officers were deciding the next move the Germans rushed the building under the cover of smoke grenades. Overwhelmed by the attack, the Hamiltons were forced back across the boulevard into the Casino. Another group of about 18 men, led by Sergeant George Hickson, managed to make it from the Casino and into the town, intent on attacking their main objective, the telephone exchange. They penetrated the narrow streets of Dieppe a little distance before they were forced back by snipers and a lack of ammunition. They cut all the telephone cables they could find and then withdrew to the Casino.

Brigadier Southam, Commander Canadian 6th Brigade, had set up his HQ in a hole scooped out of the stones, with the sea wall behind him for protection. He was the only officer of his Brigade HQ party to get ashore. Brigadier Lett, Commander Canadian 4th Brigade, never made it to the beach; the LCT carrying him had been heavily shelled and had lost all of its crew. Lett himself was seriously wounded but before losing consciousness he delegated command of his brigade to LtCol Labatt.

Trying to make some sense of the confusion, Brig Southam appraised the situation. He had received word that his men were in the Casino and this gave some cause for hope. If this success could be exploited, it might still be possible to get troops up onto the western headland.

On board the HQ ship, MajGen Roberts was receiving conflicting and sketchy reports of the situation ashore. He knew that the landings at Dieppe were in trouble, but he did not know the extent of the problem. Information supplied to him indicated that most of the enemy fire was coming from the eastern headland. Roberts therefore decided to commit his floating reserve in an attempt to silence this opposition. In consequence, les Fusiliers Mont-Royal were sent into Red Beach to help the Essex Scottish take the headland.

With the aid of smoke and in the face of fierce enemy opposition, the Mont-Royals landed at 0704hrs. German resistance had not diminished in the slightest during the 90 minutes since the first assault waves had landed. The Mont-Royals were met by hail of fire that immediately threw them into disarray. The landing craft carrying a good many of them, almost 300 men, were swept too far to the right and set down on a small, constricted beach right under the cliffs of the western headland. There they remained cut off from the battle, unable to move to the right or left, until they surrendered later that morning. The rest of the battalion suffered serious losses as soon as they reached the beach. The survivors joined with the remnants of the other two units, little more than isolated individuals struggling to stay alive and make some sense of the turmoil around them. During the course of the battle, several of these French-Canadians penetrated into the town – few returned.

On the beach things were progressively getting worse. The numbers of wounded were mounting and the ability to aid them was steadily eroding. Stretcher-bearers and medical staff were falling victim to the intense German fire. In general, the enemy seemed to be respecting the red cross flag, allowing medics to give aid to the injured unmolested. However, shells, mortar bombs and the machine-gun fire sweeping the beach killed indiscriminately whether the soldier carried a rifle or wore a red cross. Medical orderlies showed great courage working wonders on the beach that day in the most appalling conditions. Alongside them the Hamilton's padre, Capt J.W. Foote, toiled ceaselessly carrying wounded men through the bullets and mortar bombs to the aid posts and bringing comfort to the wounded and dying. Even at the end he refused an opportunity to be evacuated, preferring to join the wounded in captivity. For his valour Captain John Foote was awarded the Victoria Cross, the third to be awarded for great gallantry during the raid.

Whilst the Mont-Royals were making their attack, MajGen Roberts was considering what to do with the Royal Marine Commando. The Commando had originally been included in the raid to operate against shipping in the harbour and act as a cutting-out party to help remove German landing barges that were sheltering there. As the harbour was still in enemy hands this idea was abandoned and the Royal Marines were placed at the disposal of the Military Force Commander. Roberts decided to use them to reinforce the landings on White Beach. He

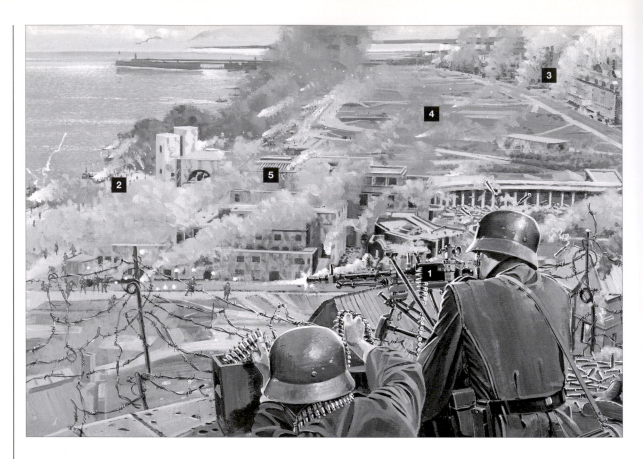

THE ATTACK ON RED AND WHITE BEACHES (pages 70–71)
German troops on the western headland overlooking
Red and White Beaches fire an MG34 (1) at those troops that
have managed to get off White Beach. The MG34 was the
standard light machine-gun used by the German Army. It
has been estimated that there were probably more MG34s
in use during the war than any other single model of gun.
Its performance was exceptional, with a rate of fire of
750 rounds per minute and a muzzle velocity of 2,750 feet
per second. (Compare this with the British Bren and the
American Browning, both with a rate of fire of 500rpm.) Its
main defect was that it was just too highly engineered; the
quality of its design called for extremely exact production
standards, which in turn led to long a manufacturing
process. Dust and grit could easily clog its finely engineered
parts and it was an expensive gun to produce, but all
of these factors were outweighed by its accuracy and
performance. The German soldiers on the Western Headland
had a perfect view of the Canadians landings over Dieppe's
Red and White Beaches (2) and the moment that the landing
craft came into range, they were met with a torrent of fire.
Although the Canadian troops desperately sought cover,
there was precious little of that to be found on the beach as
the enemy had guns covering the shore line from all angles,
including from the streets and houses of the town (3). The
wide esplanade behind the beach (4) was no better and little
more than a shooting gallery. Anyone crossing this open
grassy promenade into the town in an effort to escape the
killing ground on the shore was also vulnerable from all
directions. Those Canadian tanks that did manage to get off
the shingle and onto the grass found all the roads off the
seafront blocked by high concrete walls and covered by
machine guns. The whole area overlooked by the headland
was sealed off; tanks and men were trapped like fish in a
barrel. The Casino (5) afforded some protection to those few
Canadians of the Royal Hamilton Light Infantry that reached
it, but first the building had to be cleared of the German
troops inside it room by room. When the Casino was finally
taken there was no safe exit to the rear. That route was also
covered by machine-guns on the Western Headland. Those
who had questioned the wisdom of launching a frontal
assault against the most heavily fortified area of the
town were proved all too correct in tragic fashion.
(Howard Gerrard).

ordered LtCol Phillips to attack the western headland with his marines and help the Hamiltons and Mont-Royals to get into the town.

The Royal Marines disembarked from the *Locust* and the French 'Chasseurs', in which they had crossed the Channel, into eight landing craft. The boats moved in towards the shore accompanied by the 'Chasseurs', who laid smoke to screen them from the German shore batteries. At about 4,000 yards, the flotilla was spotted and came under shellfire that increased in intensity as the range shortened. This was soon joined by machine gun and mortar fire. Shortly afterwards, as the force came into shallow water, the 'Chasseurs' broke away leaving the small boats to complete the approach alone. As the craft left the protection of the smoke screen, it soon became clear to LtCol Phillips in the leading boat that the beach ahead of them was a complete shambles. Burning craft littered the water's edge and the shore was riddled with the bodies of the Canadians. Devastating waves of fire struck his craft and the sea all around. It was obvious to the colonel that no useful purpose could be served by continuing with the landing. At great risk to himself Phillips stood up in his boat and signalled to those following behind to abandon the landings and to make for the safety of the smoke screen. At this moment the colonel was hit and fell mortally wounded. Most craft succeeded in turning about, but

ABOVE **Major John W. Foote VC, chaplain of the Royal Hamilton Light Infantry and one of three recipients of the Victoria Cross awarded for the Dieppe raid. He won his award for his bravery attending to the dead and the wounded on Red and White Beaches. He declined the offer to be evacuated and went into captivity with his men. (National Archives of Canada, PA-501320)**

ABOVE, LEFT **Warships in action off Dieppe, firing on the eastern headland to the left of the harbour entrance. Royal Navy destroyers came close inshore on many occasions to engage targets on the eastern headland, but were always forced to retire by the enemy gun batteries behind Dieppe. (Imperial War Museum, A11232)**

LEFT **The casualties were heavy on practically every beach. Here some Canadian wounded lie on the beach at Dieppe beside a knocked-out Churchill tank. In the background smoke drifts over the battlefield from a deserted and immobilised landing craft tank. (Bundesarchiv, 101/292/1205/14)**

two missed the signal and pressed on to make their landing. All of the marines in those craft were killed, wounded or captured; none returned.

After witnessing the demise of the Royal Marine Commando, the senior officer in charge of the 'Chasseurs' signalled to HMS *Calpe* giving details of the debacle. Around 0915hrs MajGen Roberts was informed that the position on Red and White Beaches was out of control. With all his forces committed there was nothing more that could be done, Roberts prepared to admit defeat.

THE GERMAN REACTION

The raid on Dieppe had achieved tactical surprise. Contrary to many opinions expressed later, the Germans were not expecting the attack. The first indication that something was afoot was when the flotilla of small craft taking 3 Commando to Berneval ran into the German convoy. The sound of this naval action was picked up ashore and by three harbour lookout ships stationed off Dieppe. This was deemed sufficiently significant for an alert to be issued to local coastal commands.

At first the action was thought to be one of the usual attacks made on convoys through the Channel. While this was being investigated, reports came into GenLt Konrad Haase's Divisional HQ at Envermu that landings were being made at Berneval and Quiberville. A few minutes later news arrived of the bombardment of the seafront at Dieppe and of British fighters attacking the east and west headlands. A short while later there was news of more landings at Pourville and Puys. Haase's first thoughts were that it was a commando raid, then, with the reports of landings multiplying, he became convinced that it was the invasion. These events were signalled up the chain of command and were recorded at German 15th Army HQ at 0530hrs. Opinion was divided as it was still not clear whether this was an invasion or a raid of a more local nature. Nevertheless, 30 minutes later it was thought proper to alert the 15th Army reserves. 10th Panzer Division, the *Leibstandarte SS Adolf Hitler* Division and 7th Luftwaffe Division were warned to be prepared. At 0700hrs 15th Army's Chief of Staff alerted Berlin. Hitler's Chief of General Staff, General der Artillerie Alfred Jodl, was told that the enemy had landed in strength and the appropriate measures had been taken by 15th Army. It was explained that counterattacks were being made by local reserves and an alert had been passed to Army reserves.

At 0715hrs Gen Kuntzen at LXXXI Corps HQ informed 15th Army HQ that he judged the enemy operation to be a local action that was being dealt with by local reserves. However, GFM von Rundstedt, CinC (West) thought it prudent to warn all army and air force commands that the landings might be a diversion for other landings elsewhere and urged the utmost vigilance. At 0750hrs Kuntzen asked 3rd Air Squadron for air support against enemy naval vessels but requested that there be no aerial intervention in the fighting on land. Air reconnaissance was also requested to sweep the Channel looking for enemy reinforcements at sea.

Closer to the action, the commander of 302nd Infantry had already started to deploy his reserves. Major Blücher was ordered to assemble a force to counterattack the landings at Berneval. At Puys the local units there related that the enemy landing had been contained and that none

Within a very short time of the initial assault landings on the beach at Dieppe the area was a scene of total death and destruction. This picture taken after the raid gives some idea of the carnage wreaked during the battle. This is a slightly different view of the tank shown on p.73 (National Archives of Canada, C-14160)

of the invasion force had got off the beach. There was no news about the landings at Quiberville and communications with the gun battery at Varengeville had been lost. Then came news of the attack on Dieppe. Haase realised he was facing landings along a front of 11 miles from Quiberville to Berneval, but decided to rely on local units to contain the assault until things became clearer. He did not want to move too soon.

For a while things began to look black for the 302nd Division. Varengeville battery radioed that they were being attacked. News also arrived that Pourville had been taken and that enemy troops were advancing on the radar station and Quatre Vents Farm, but the situation in Dieppe looked good. Few troops were off the beach and the tanks that had landed were bottled up on the seafront. Realising that the Pourville landings posed the greatest threat, Haase dispatched the cyclist company from Gueures and the anti-tank platoon and infantry gun platoon of the 371st Regiment from Offranville to Petit Appeville to hold the bridge over the Scie and cover Quatre Vents Farm from the rear. He also ordered a strong patrol from Ouville to support the battery at Varengeville.

By 0600hrs things looked as though they were beginning to settle down. The defences at Dieppe were holding, none of the enemy forces were off of the beach at Puys and the situation at Berneval was stable. Haase's main worry was his left flank at Pourville and Varengeville. When, a little later, he heard a strong force of the enemy was advancing up the Scie valley from Pourville, he decided to commit his main reserve. Haase sent 1st Battalion, 571st Regiment from Ouville towards the landings at Pourville, ordering one half to swing left down the valley to Pourville, while the remainder linked up with the anti-tank company at Petit Appeville. He also sent the 302nd Anti-Tank Company into Dieppe. With these measures he was confident he could stabilise the situation.

General Adolf Kuntzen at LXXXI Corps was concerned with the wider picture. To back up Haase's forces, he ordered forward two battalions from the 676th Infantry Regiment from the neighbouring 336th Division to consolidate around Offranville and act as a further reserve should a breakthrough by the enemy be made. Everyone now looked to the 302nd Division to see if it could contain the landings. As things turned out, it was more than capable of doing just that.

THE AIR AND
SEA BATTLES

When news of the scale of the raid on Dieppe was first given to the RAF it was greeted with delight. It provided a long-awaited opportunity of taking on the Luftwaffe in France and inflicting some serious damage. By August 1942 the greater part of the Luftwaffe's fighting strength was concentrated on the Eastern Front against Russia, assisting the German Army in its summer offensive. Northern France, Belgium and the Netherlands were held by Luftflotte 3, commanded by GFM Hugo Sperrle. Luftflotte 3 under Sperrle had taken part in the campaigns in the Low Countries and northern France in 1940, the Battle of Britain and the subsequent 'Blitz' against Britain. In the spring of 1941 the bulk of its flying units had been transferred to the East to participate in the attack upon the Soviet Union. Since then Sperrle's mighty force had been further weakened and during 1942 it was only capable of minor bombing attacks against the UK and modest interdictory flights against Allied intruders. Its main strength now lay in just two fighter and two bomber geschwaders. Jagdgeschwader 2 and Jagdgeschwader 26 each contained three Gruppen with a total nominal strength of 90 fighters. Each of the two bomber geschwaders, Kampfgeschwader 2 and Kampfgeschwader 40, also included three Gruppen and a nominal strength of 90 bombers. These were supplemented by training and reconnaissance units. Both the fighter and bomber units were often below their full complement because of a lack of trained aircrews and some aircraft being unserviceable. Luftflotte 3's low operational strength required that it husband its resources and this led to a certain reticence to engage in major air battles.

This declining power of the Luftwaffe in France was in marked contrast to the growing strength of the RAF. Since the Battle of Britain, the RAF had evolved into a very powerful force, equipped with increasing numbers of skilled pilots and modern aircraft. It had taken the fight back to Germany with nightly bombing raids against its towns and industrial plants, secured the skies above Britain with new squadrons of day and night fighters and roamed at will across the northern part of the Continent with daylight attacks. But it could not bring the Luftwaffe to battle. Skirmishes were fought and losses were inflicted and suffered on both sides, but the scale of the actions were always relatively minor. The Dieppe raid would fill the sea off the coast of France with shipping and thousands of Allied troops; this was a target that the Luftwaffe could not ignore. Luftflotte 3 and its fighter and bomber groups would have to come out and fight and, this time, the RAF would be ready for them.

The Air Battle

The Air Force Commander for the Dieppe raid was Air Vice-Marshal Leigh-Mallory. He led Fighter Command's No. 11 Group, which controlled the whole of south-east England. For the raid, No. 11 Group had under

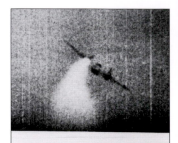

View from the RAF Spitfire of a Norwegian sergeant pilot as he attacks a Dornier Do 17 above Dieppe. The bomber is hit in the port engine and begins to burn. Moments later the aircraft crashed into the sea. (Imperial War Museum, C3195)

command 46 Spitfire, 8 Hurricane, 3 Typhoon and 4 Mustang fighter squadrons and 7 Boston and Blenheim bomber squadrons. A force of this size had not been brought together for one operation since the Battle of Britain two years previously.

The Boston and Blenheim aircraft from No. 2 Group Bomber Command would bomb and lay smoke in support of the troop landings. The Hurricanes were to be used as fighter-bombers, attacking ground targets with cannon fire and heavier ordnance. The Mustangs would provide tactical reconnaissance, not only over the battlefield but also over an area further inland to spot any German troop movements towards the landing areas. The 49 squadrons of Spitfires were to provide the air umbrella for the landings, mounting patrols ready to pounce on any enemy aircraft that interfered with the operation. Each Spitfire squadron would be expected to patrol over the area for at least 30 minutes, 60 miles away from the English coast and often over 100 miles from their bases. For the relatively short-ranged Spitfires this could be a serious problem. These squadrons would often have to be grouped together in wing strength, overlapping with each other to ensure a permanent numerical advantage over the enemy. It was stressed that failure to maintain this air superiority could cost the attacking force dearly.

The crews of the Bostons of 107, 605 and 418 Squadrons were the first airmen to be issued orders, in the early hours of 19 August. At 0306hrs they were ordered to attack the German gun batteries Hitler and Göring at 0445hrs, just as the flank attacks were going in. Other units were briefed in rapid succession. Hurricanes of 3, 32, 43, 245 and 253 Squadrons were to attack the headlands either side of Dieppe at 0515hrs. Spitfires of 129 Squadron were to attack the Hess Battery observation post at Pointe d'Ailly at 0445hrs. Spitfires from 65 and 111 squadrons were ordered to provide escort patrols, to cover the bombing attacks. And so it went on. As

Canadian troops, many of them wounded, returning to their mother ship during the raid. (National Archives of Canada, PA-116298)

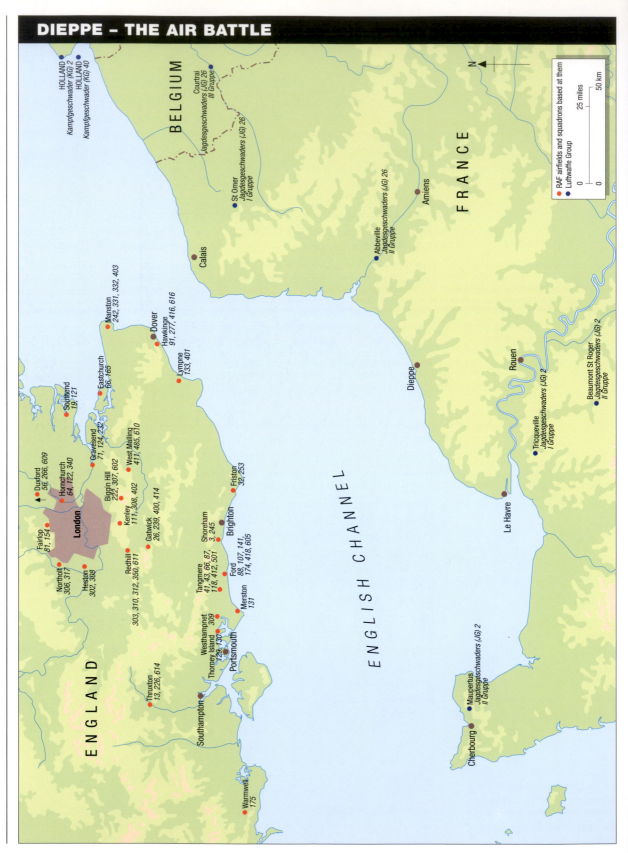

HOLLAND
Kampfgeschwader (KG) 2
HOLLAND
Kampfgeschwader (KG) 40

BELGIUM

Courtrai
*Jagdesgeschwaders (JG) 26
III Gruppe*

St Omer
*Jagdesgeschwaders (JG) 26
I Gruppe*

Calais

Manston
242, 331, 332, 403

Dover

Hawkinge
91, 277, 416, 616

Lympne
133, 401

Eastchurch
66, 165

Southend
19, 121

Gravesend
71, 124, 232

West Malling
411, 485, 610

Duxford
56, 266, 609

Hornchurch
64, 122, 340

Biggin Hill
222, 307, 602

Kenley
111, 308, 402

Gatwick
26, 239, 400, 414

Friston
32, 253

Shoreham
3, 245

Brighton

London

Fairlop
81, 154

Northolt
306, 317

Heston
302, 308

Redhill
303, 310, 312, 350, 611

Tangmere
*41, 43, 66, 87,
118, 412, 501*

Ford
*88, 107, 141,
174, 418, 605*

Merston
131

Westhampnet
129, 130

Thorney Island
309

Portsmouth

Thruxton
13, 226, 614

Southampton

Warmwell
175

FRANCE

Amiens

Abbeville
*Jagdesgeschwaders (JG) 26
II Gruppe*

Dieppe

Rouen

Beaumont St Roger
*Jagdesgeschwaders (JG) 2
II Gruppe*

Tricqueville
*Jagdesgeschwaders (JG) 2
I Gruppe*

Le Havre

Maupertus
*Jagdesgeschwaders (JG) 2
II Gruppe*

Cherbourg

ENGLAND

ENGLISH CHANNEL

N

50 km
25 miles
0
0

● RAF airfields and squadrons based at them
● Luftwaffe Group

Wounded Canadians being landed from a British destroyer after the raid. Casualty evacuation was a difficult operation as all the landing craft going to and from the beaches were under continual enemy fire. Many of the wounded who were safely put into craft for evacuation were killed later during the passage out to the warships when these craft were sunk. (National Archives of Canada, PA-113248

the troops neared the beaches and dawn lit the sky, more and more RAF aircraft took off to join the battle.

The results of the first bombing raids were disappointing. None of the German gun batteries were put out of action and few of the weapons on the headlands were destroyed. The smoke laid by the bombers was effective, at least temporarily, and did give some measure of protection during the initial assault but soon dispersed in a light breeze. The only resistance the Allied airmen encountered was relatively inaccurate German anti-aircraft fire. The bombing and strafing runs by the Hurricane squadrons cost them eight aircraft, with 20 damaged, four seriously. These early missions over Dieppe encountered no German aircraft at all. Enemy fighters were slow to scramble because of early morning mist over their airfields and absent aircrews. At about 0700hrs, with the landings already two hours old, the first enemy fighters were encountered when Focke-Wulf Fw 190s and Messerschmitt BF 109s clashed with the Spitfires patrolling high above the warships. Dogfights erupted that would continue throughout the day.

The Luftwaffe had the advantage of operating close to their bases and could therefore remain in the air above Dieppe for longer periods. They could also land and refuel much more swiftly. The result was that, for most of the day, the numbers of Luftwaffe aircraft were roughly equal to those of the RAF machines pitted against them. They had a further advantage, for the majority of these aircraft were Fw 190s, a fighter with a much higher performance than that of the Spitfire. Leigh-Mallory failed to achieve the

marked numerical superiority he had hoped to have over Dieppe during the battle, and his pilots suffered accordingly.

German bombers were much slower to arrive on the scene than their fighters. The need to arm and fuel these unprepared aircraft meant that they did not appear over Dieppe until after 0900hrs, when they were directed at the ships off the coast and attacked in waves protected by fighters. Soon afterwards, at around 0930hrs, radar stations on the English coast began to record increased air activity in northern France as German units from more far-flung airfields began to arrive in the skies above Dieppe. Fighter aircraft and bombers from the whole of Luftflotte 3, from Normandy, Belgium and the Netherlands homed in on the battle. By 1000hrs no ship was safe from attack and no British fighter was ever alone in the sky. Both sides suffered substantial losses as attacks were pressed home with great determination. Most of the ships off the coast were attacked and suffered at least some damage. The sky was full of weaving aircraft chasing each other amid streams of coloured tracer. Anti-aircraft fire snaked up from the ships as lumbering twin-engined Dorniers began their bombing runs. The RAF had got its wish – the Luftwaffe had been drawn into battle and it was giving a very good account of itself.

The Sea Battle

Like the RAF, the Royal Navy had both an offensive and a defensive role in the operation. The Navy's primary task was to transport and land the attacking force on the shores of France, but it was also to aid that

A disabled Churchill tank which had one of its tracks blown off whilst trying to cross the shingle bank at the top of Red Beach. It had forced its way through the first belt of wire only to come to grief in front of the sea wall. Although potentially still capable of continuing the fight, it could not elevate its main gun sufficiently to bring it to bear on the enemy. The crew abandoned the tank. (Bundesarchiv, 101/362/2209/14)

force in attacking the enemy. The naval guns were supposed to be the primary means with which to bombard, and hopefully eliminate, German defences. What the naval force lacked in large-calibre guns would be more than made up for with numbers. The Naval Force Commander, Capt Hughes-Hallet, had 237 craft at his disposal for the operation, most of which were coastal vessels and landing craft.

The Royal Navy's first clash with the enemy was when the craft carrying 3 Commando ran into the German convoy. Strangely these German ships were not detected by the radar of any vessel in the operation, although shore-based radar in England had picked up the enemy convoy as early as 0040hrs and passed a warning to the Naval Force Commander at least an hour before contact was made. The destroyers *Slazak* and *Brocklesby*, who were the operation's port side guard ships, took no part in the subsequent action, although they witnessed the battle from a distance of four miles without realising the significance of what they were seeing. It was presumed that the firing they could see was coming from ashore. It was left to a flak ship and a motor gunboat to deal with the enemy and, as described above, the consequences were quite disastrous.

Once in their various assembly positions, the infantry landing ships lowered their assault landing craft and the troops embarked ready for the run to shore. It was here that various small craft gave their support. Motor launches navigated and escorted the troop-carrying assault boats into their landing beaches, steam gun boats gave protection to the flanks, landing craft support (LCS) provided close fire support to the landings themselves and landing craft flak (LCF) kept watch for enemy aircraft and fired on known gun positions. Following close behind the armada of small boats came the bombarding force of the Hunt-class destroyers. Once the assault force had landed these craft remained on call during the day to give support as requested. Unfortunately, in most cases communications with the shore were nonexistent and the ships were left to attack targets of opportunity or known enemy defence points.

Support for the landings on Red and White Beaches came from one of the flak ships, LCF(L) 2, which fought with great gallantry. Her captain brought her close inshore to fire at the German defences at almost point-blank range. She continued giving support until she was disabled, her captain killed and her guns put out of action. Dead in the water she was battered by shellfire until she finally sank. The *Locust* also joined in this bombardment, arriving off Red Beach at 0530hrs near the harbour entrance and opening fire with her 4in. gun. She soon came under accurate fire from the heavy batteries inland and from the guns on the eastern headland. At 0611hrs she received a direct hit to her bridge and withdrew.

The destroyers also gave supporting fire during the morning but the accuracy of their bombardment was variable. The Forward Observation Officers who had landed with the assault troops and were intended to identify targets and give corrections to the destroyers, had either become casualties or were unable to communicate back to the warships. The *Albrighton* did manage to silence an anti-aircraft battery above Pourville, but other positive successes were few. Their guns were just not powerful enough to do the necessary damage. The *Bleasdale* engaged a battery on the cliffs to the east of Dieppe and the *Garth* bombarded positions on the eastern headland, but both were unable to silence their targets.

DOGFIGHT OVER DIEPPE (pages 82–83)

Two Spitfires from 610 Squadron are attacked by Focke-Wulf Fw 190s, 9,000ft above the beach at Dieppe. The leading Spitfire with the identification code DW-D (1) is flown by Pilot Officer L.E. Hokem. A short while previously he had engaged an Fw 190 and blasted pieces off its tailplane, but now other 190s are closing on him. A few seconds later a burst of fire from a German fighter hits and severely damages Hokem's Spitfire, but he manages to disengage and get his aircraft safely home. The other Spitfire, DW-F (2), piloted by Flight Lieutenant Peter Poole was not so lucky. His aircraft was completely destroyed in the encounter and crashed into the sea killing F/Lt Poole. The German aircraft (3) are from II Gruppe, Jagdesgeschwader (JG) 26 based at Abbeville. Jagdesgeschwader 26 was a day-fighter unit. The term Geschwader was used for the largest flying unit in the Luftwaffe to have a fixed nominal strength. It contained three Gruppe each with a total of 30 aircraft. Later in the war these numbers were increased. JG26 was one of only two fighter Geschwaders in France in 1942 and its aircraft were based to the east of the Seine. The other was JG2 based to the west of the river. The commander of II Gruppe JG26 was Oberleutnant Wilhelm-Ferdinand 'Wutz' Galland, brother of the German ace Adolf Galland. At the time of Dieppe, 'Wutz' Galland had 12 victories to his credit. The Fw 190s flown by JG26 totally outclassed the Spitfire Vs flown by 610 Squadron. It was faster, could out-climb and out-dive the RAF fighter and had a more powerful armament. The Spitfire's only advantage was that it had a tighter turn. This difference in performance between the two fighters cost Fighter Command high losses during the early months of 1942. In March 32 Spitfires were destroyed, then 103 in April and 61 in May. This situation continued until the Spitfire Mk. IX came into service in the summer of 1942 and then the RAF was able to operate on nearly equal terms. The Mk. IX was similar to the Mk. V, but had a strengthened engine mounting and rear fuselage to hold the new Merlin 61 Series engine. The Mk. IXs were almost impossible to distinguish from the Mk. Vs, which was very disconcerting for Fw 190 pilots! Eventually 5,665 Mk IXs were built, more than any other mark of Spitfire. Only four of the squadrons at Dieppe had Mk. IX Spitfires. The remaining 42 squadrons had the less powerful Mk. V and VI versions of the fighter. During the Dieppe raid, Spitfires flew 2,050 sorties with 59 aircraft lost to enemy action.

(Howard Gerrard)

Fast steam gunboats repeatedly swept the flanks of this small armada guarding against any enemy interference from the sea. During one of these sweeps SGB 8 and 9 came under attack from enemy aircraft. A formation of Fw 190s attacked the vessels and SGB 9 was disabled, but both boats managed to return towards Dieppe after some running repairs. These SGBs saw nothing, but a report was received by *Calpe* whilst they were out on the sweep that German E-boats were approaching from Boulogne. The *Slazak, Brocklesby* and *Bleasdale* were despatched to intercept, but the report proved to be false. These destroyers had to leave the fighter screen to attend to the report and were subsequently set upon by German fighters. They were subjected to numerous attacks, but only *Slazak* was hit, suffering superficial damage.

The landing craft that had landed their complement on Dieppe beach and elsewhere withdrew a few miles out to sea. An area of sea had been designated the 'Boat Pool' and it was here that the craft could be held in readiness until they received the order for the post-operation evacuation of troops from the beaches. The area was continually shrouded in a blanket of smoke that kept it relatively safe from the coastal batteries and German aircraft.

DISASTER, WITHDRAWAL AND SURRENDER

By 0815hrs the one successful action of Operation Jubilee, the destruction of Hess Battery by the men of Lord Lovat's 4 Commando, had been completed. 4 Commando had now re-embarked and were on their way home. All along the coast behind them, from Pourville to Berneval, a tragedy was unfolding. At that time the troops of 3 Commando were fighting for their existence against Blücher Force, ultimately to be captured or killed. This awful fate was also about to overwhelm most of the Canadians fighting on the other Jubilee beaches.

At Puys the destiny of the troops of the Royal Regiment trapped on the beach was abundantly clear. They would either have to surrender or die. There appeared to be no other option. Ahead of them the towering sea wall topped by impenetrable wire barred the exit from the beach, behind them the sea was empty of craft and enemy fire poured down on them from every side. From time to time a few men summoned the courage to make a dash for the sea in a desperate attempt to swim to freedom. Most were shot but a few escaped, the lucky ones picked up out at sea by friendly craft. The vast majority of the Royals, however, clung tightly to their exposed refuge and waited for the madness to end.

Since the third wave had arrived on Blue Beach at 0545hrs few other craft had been able to even approach the shore. At 0700hrs a message was received by the HQ ship HMS *Calpe* asking for all landing craft to go to Puys to evacuate the beach party. Two craft picked up the request only one of which, LCA 209, was an assault landing craft. This boat went in but was immediately half swamped by a rush of soldiers. She tried to back off, but was hit by an enemy shell and sank 50 yards out. Only two of her crew and one soldier survived.

The eastern end of Green Beach looking towards Dieppe. On the right is the high ground up which LtCol Merritt VC and his South Saskatchewans attacked trying to capture the radar station and get on to the rear of the western headland that overlooks Dieppe. The large broken structure on the beach in the lower centre of the picture is part of that German radar station. It has collapsed down onto the shore through cliff erosion. (Ken Ford)

Later that morning the destroyer *Garth* picked up a plaintive message asking for help and evacuation. At 1100hrs some craft approached the beach but were forced back by enemy fire. They reported to *Calpe* that they could see no one on the beach. Another attempt was made soon afterwards with the same result and the same message. Only the dead remained on the beach – The Royal Regiment of Canada had surrendered.

On Green Beach, at Pourville, the South Saskatchewans and the Cameron Highlanders were feeling the effects of the German reinforcements being introduced into the battle. Lieutenant-Colonel Merritt and his Saskatchewans had been fought to a standstill on the rear on the eastern hills above Pourville. His men had braved incredibly heavy enemy fire to push forward, but each small gain was followed by a painful and costly withdrawal. With new German troops and weapons arriving by the minute, his force was in great danger of being completely overrun.

Major Law of the Camerons had been frustrated in his attempt to reach Petit Appeville by the arrival of German reinforcements securing the strategically important bridge over the River Scie. He had reached the area at 0845hrs and waited for the supporting tanks that should have arrived from Dieppe, but none came. By 0930hrs he knew that his mission to advance on the airfield at St Aubin was now impossible. More immediately pressing to him was the arrival of men of the German 1st Battalion, 571st Infantry Regiment, who were coming down the road from Ouville and crossing his front just a few hundred yards ahead of him. The time had come to make a withdrawal to the beach. Law gave the order and his men began a rearguard action to extricate themselves from their exposed salient. Almost immediately a signal was received from the Military Force Commander ordering the evacuation from Green Beach at 1000hrs.

The increasingly gloomy messages arriving at MajGen Roberts' HQ from the beaches had left him with no option but to issue the order to withdraw. The lack of information coming from the beaches suggested things had gone badly wrong, and those few that were received painted a stark picture of failure and death. At around 0900hrs the Military Force Commander concluded that his troops on Red and White Beaches were unlikely to capture the headlands to the east and west of Dieppe and that

The scout car 'Hunter' abandoned during the battle. It was disabled by a tank reversing into it and not by enemy fire. Throughout the battle, its crew were able to use its radio to stay in contact with the HQ ship HMS *Calpe* at sea. For part of the time Brig Southam, Commander Canadian 4th Brigade, used this car as his brigade's communications centre. The Casino and the disabled LCT 159 can just be made out in the background. (National Archives of Canada, C-29861)

the main assault had failed. Landing the remaining tanks of the Calgary Regiment that he was keeping in reserve would, he knew, be useless. It was time to salvage what he could from the disaster. He ordered the troop withdrawal to start at 1030hrs. An RAF advisor questioned this decision, pointing out that the timing would upset the original RAF timetable and might make it impossible to give adequate air support and to lay the smoke screen. The evacuation was finally arranged for 1100hrs. Orders were sent by the Naval Force Commander to all LCAs to return to their original landing beaches to take the men off. The original plan had envisaged that troops on Red and White Beaches would be taken off by LCTs, but this idea was now abandoned in view of the strength of enemy artillery fire. The larger craft were much too vulnerable. The LCAs would have to ferry the men out to the LCTs who would wait offshore.

The troops on Green Beach had believed that the evacuation would start at 1000hrs as a signal had already been received to this effect. The subsequent delay until 1100hrs meant the South Saskatchewans and Camerons would have to contend with an increasingly vigorous enemy for an extra hour. The delay proved disastrous for the Canadians. The Camerons had already begun to fall back to the beach at 0930hrs, withdrawing down the Scie valley to Green Beach. The isolated companies of the Saskatchewans also began to shrink their exposed perimeter, prior to embarkation. By the time the troops were made aware of the change of plan and consequent delay, the lodgement was too small to be defensively viable. The enemy had been allowed to close on the surviving troops too long before the withdrawal. For the next hour the two besieged battalions had to fight off repeated attacks. The entire beachhead was now overlooked by German troops and snipers and machine gunners had a field day. Individuals were picked off and groups were mortared where they sheltered. In the hours before the order to withdraw was given the Saskatchewans and Camerons had lost roughly 20 per cent of their men. In that last hour before the landing craft came to attempt to rescue them their losses mounted to 40 per cent.

At 1045hrs six LCAs came inshore to Green Beach under very heavy fire. It was a mistake, the craft should have gone into Red Beach to start the evacuation there, but got lost in the smoke and arrived at Pourville. The destroyers *Albrighton* and *Bleasdale* covered the rescue attempt by bombarding the flanks and firing smoke shells. Troops ashore rushed out to meet the boats, wading through the surf trying to avoid enemy fire. This slowed the landing craft as they had to pick the men out of the water one by one. Once beached there was another rush for the craft. Men toppled into the boats and into the sea, cut down by enemy fire. The dead and the wounded jammed the ramps; some craft were heavily overloaded and shipped water. As quickly as they could the boat crews reversed off the beach and attempted to get out into the open sea. One craft was sunk during the withdrawal and tipped all of its men in the water. Those LCAs that did manage to get out transferred their troops onto destroyers. Some craft returned to Green Beach to try again, whilst others carried out their original orders and went on to Red Beach. At 1100hrs four more landing craft went into Pourville. Again the German fire picked off men running down the beach to the craft and mortars and shellfire raked the boats. Of the four assault boats that landed LCA 317 was hit and abandoned, LCA 251 was overloaded and sank 250 yards

The Churchill tank 'Cat' made it from the beach onto the esplanade and motored up and down trying to find an exit into the town, but it was unable to penetrate into the side streets because of roadblocks. For the next two hours it moved backwards and forwards along the sea front firing its machine guns and main weapon. It was eventually knocked out by a Ju-87 'Stuka' dive-bomber. (Bundesarchiv, 101/MW6379/36)

out and LCA 214 and LCA 262 both made it away from the beach, but sank alongside the destroyers *Albrighton* and *Bleasdale* after they had transferred their troops.

For the next 30 minutes several other LCAs came into Green Beach to take a few more men away. By 1130hrs only LtCol Merritt and about 100 men remained as a rearguard around the perimeter of the beach. They tried to set fire to the houses in Pourville to provide some cover for their withdrawal, but this proved impossible. Trapped in the last few houses, Merritt and his men were finally overwhelmed by the enemy. These last brave Saskatchewans and Camerons were forced to surrender and were made prisoners. At 1215hrs a lone LCA came close into Green Beach and reported no one left alive. It withdrew under heavy enemy fire.

The chaos and death of the withdrawal from Green Beach was mirrored by the events on Red and White Beaches. The Casino opposite Red Beach was still held by the Canadians, but the enemy were pressing hard to retake the strongpoint. Brigadier Southam knew that once the Casino fell the whole of the shoreline would be untenable. At 1020hrs a line of destroyers followed some LCAs in towards Dieppe, laying a smoke screen. A little later, between 1100hrs and 1200hrs, RAF aircraft flew continual sorties low over the headlands laying smoke. The smoke proved a double-edged weapon, however, effectively shielding the landing craft until they were close in shore but hiding the beaches from the destroyers, reducing the effectiveness of their covering fire.

At 1020hrs the Flotilla Officer (FO) of the LSI *Prince Charles* went in to Red Beach with eight of his LCAs. Six of these craft were destroyed, including that of the Flotilla Officer: the remaining two managed to rescue a few troops. Next came the craft from the LSI *Princess Astrid*. Four LCAs with their FO went in to White Beach. On touching down, the craft were swamped by the weight of men trying to get on board. One craft was hit by a shell and sank. The other three managed to extricate about 70 men each but two of these later sank out at sea. From his position in the Casino, Brig Southam could see the landing craft running this gauntlet of fire and the casualties on the beach. He decided the time had come to abandon the Casino and make for the beach. As the Canadians withdrew the Germans were practically on their heels.

As Southam knew, the loss of the Casino meant the beach could no longer be held. Soldiers along the promenade and the sea wall began

surrendering to the enemy crossing over the gardens onto the lateral road. At 1100hrs the FO of the LSI *Glengyle* went into White Beach with three craft of his flotilla and two from the *Prince Charles*. By then most of the beach was in enemy hands. A small pocket of Canadians was grouped around a disabled LCT and some of these made it into the LCAs. Many were killed later during the withdrawal.

Soon after this the Naval Force Commander realised that the position ashore was hopeless and that increasing enemy fire had made it too hazardous for any further rescue attempts. *Brocklesby, Fernie* and *Locust* were still close inshore bombarding targets on the headlands and receiving fire in return. At 1215hrs *Brocklesby* signalled that the only life seen on the beach was the group of Canadians sheltering behind the stranded LCT and it would be impossible for anyone to close on the beach and get them out. At 1220hrs *Calpe* ordered all further evacuation attempts to cease. By this time around 400 men had been brought off Red and White Beaches, the remainder were either dead or captive.

At 1240hrs Captain Hughes-Hallet and MajGen Roberts ran HMS *Calpe* close inshore off Red Beach for a final inspection. In defiance she opened fire with her 4in. guns, bombarding the German positions on the headlands. No troops could be seen on the beach; it was all over. The *Calpe* made smoke and retired out to sea.

With the land battle over the sea and air battle continued. The naval force, strung out over tens of miles, was attacked all the way across the Channel by enemy aircraft. The sky overhead was criss-crossed by vapour trails and tracer fire as the Spitfires fought off the Luftwaffe to keep them from the ships down below. Three Dorniers did, however, get through to one of the destroyers and one bomber managed to drop its load on the *Berkeley*. The warship was hit twice on the starboard side just forward of the bridge. The bombs broke the ship's back and she began to sink. The destroyer was abandoned and SGB 8 took off her crew. HMS *Albrighton* sank her later with a torpedo.

AFTERMATH AND LESSONS LEARNED

Despite the great acts of bravery and the professional and determined conduct of the servicemen involved in Operation Jubilee the raid has to be seen as a disaster. On the face of it Jubilee achieved little, for almost none of the original objectives were achieved and the cost in human lives was disastrous.

The 'butcher's bill' for the raid was horrific. Of the 6,000 men who took part in the landings, 2,078 returned to England, of whom 850 never landed at all. The Canadians lost 56 officers and 906 other ranks killed. Total losses for the Canadians were 3,367 killed, wounded and captured. The Commandos suffered 270 killed, wounded or captured. In the nine hours of the battle the Canadians lost more prisoners than they would in 20 months of action in Italy. The Royal Navy suffered 550 casualties. Losses suffered by the enemy were just over 600. Of these, the army had 333 killed, wounded and missing (132 dead), the navy lost 113 casualties killed, wounded and missing (78 dead) and the Luftwaffe's losses, including ground personnel, were 162 killed and wounded (104 dead).

In its attempt to inflict a bloody defeat on the Luftwaffe, the RAF actually came off worst numerically. Although it claimed 91 victories and 44 probable kills, German records show they lost 48 aircraft, including those destroyed on the ground, with 24 others damaged. In reply the RAF admitted to 106 losses due to enemy action and 14 other aircraft written off because of damage. The human cost to the RAF was 67 pilots killed. The losses suffered by the Luftwaffe may have been lower than those of the British but their impact was greater due to the smaller size of the enemy air fleets stationed in France. The loss of 48 aircraft and their pilots was a great blow to the effectiveness of the German Air Force on the other side of the Channel.

When the news of the raid was released to the people of Canada it was met with a wave of euphoria. People were thrilled to learn that Canadians had been in action in France. This feeling soon evaporated when details of the casualties were reported. The defeat and great loss of life also sent ripples through the establishment in England and people quickly began to distance themselves from the responsibility for the failure. Churchill thought that the plan was ill-conceived and was puzzled by Allied tactics, as indeed were the Germans. Generalleutnant Konrad Haase later said, 'The main reason that the Canadians did not gain any ground on the beaches was not due to any lack of courage, but because of the concentrated defensive fire.' He found it incomprehensible that the Canadians were ordered to attack head-on against a German infantry regiment supported by artillery, without sufficient naval and air co-operation to suppress the defences. All in all he found the plan of attack to be 'mediocre'.

The Germans quite naturally made great propaganda out of the debacle, demonstrating to the world the superiority of German defences and the inferiority of Allied tactics. The huge numbers of prisoners taken at Dieppe, filmed and photographed as they walked dejectedly into captivity, made sombre viewing. The enemy also revelled in pictures of the abandoned armour and equipment that was scattered over the beaches including Britain's latest tank, the Churchill. One of the most valuable items left on the beach was the plans for Operation Jubilee hurriedly abandoned by Brig Southam. A complete set of plans left on the beach by the commander of 4th Brigade, allowed the Germans to examine the whole of the operation in detail, from conception to exploitation. It was a great coup for German intelligence.

Ironically, this great German victory eventually contributed to their ultimate defeat. Although the losses had proved dreadful, much was in fact gained by the Allies, for the lessons learned at Dieppe helped pave the way for victory when the Allies returned to France in earnest.

Conversely, flushed with their success, the German High Command drew dangerous conclusions from Operation Jubilee. They saw the action at Dieppe as a vindication of their chosen strategy to repel a seaborne invasion. The tactics that had brought success at Dieppe would remain the basis of the defence of not just Normandy but the whole coastline of occupied Europe. Strong, fixed defences had stopped the Allies on the beaches at Dieppe and Hitler and his generals believed that this was how any future invasion could be stopped. The Führer ordered a strengthening of the coastal defences all along the North Sea, Channel and Atlantic seaboards, creating an impregnable 'Atlantic Wall' against which his enemies would dash themselves to pieces. This defensive mentality, at the expense of mobility and flexibility, ultimately played into the hands of the Allies.

The Allies in contrast learned a little more from the raid. Their experience at Dieppe taught them that, even if they could successfully storm a defended port, the cost would be prohibitive. So when Operation Overlord was implemented they pragmatically took their ports with them, in the shape of two gigantic artificial 'Mulberry' harbours. Dieppe also demonstrated that cooperation between the three services would have to be much more closely integrated to successfully execute any large-scale amphibious operation. New techniques and armour would have to be developed to attack fixed defences and tanks would have to land simultaneously with the assaulting infantry. Heavy naval and air bombardment would have to precede any attack and close support from large-calibre weapons would be essential immediately prior to any landings. Airborne forces would be needed to seize and hold vital positions behind enemy lines ahead of the landings to halt, or at least seriously disrupt, the flow of reinforcements to the landing area. Probably the single most important lesson of Operation Jubilee was that a much larger fleet of landing craft of all types and sizes would be vital to enable the Allies to put a strong force ashore in one lift. It is to the credit of the Allied High Command that these lessons were taken to heart and the rewards were reaped a thousandfold on the morning of 6 June 1944 on another group of Normandy beaches.

THE BATTLEFIELD TODAY

The Dieppe raid's battlefield stretches along the north-east coastline of Normandy, never straying more than a mile from the sea. All eight landing beaches, each dramatic in its own way, can be visited comfortably in a day. Some, like Quiberville and Dieppe, are wide, open expanses of shingle, flanked by roads and houses. Others are cramped and sandy, dominated by sheer chalk cliffs.

Dieppe is now a bustling port and holiday resort, with many visitor attractions. An open grassy promenade still stretches behind what were Red and White Beaches, lined by the hotels and other buildings of the Boulevard de Verdun just as it was in 1942. The location of the Casino is marked by monuments and plaques although the building has been replaced by a car park and swimming pool. A brass tablet commemorates the US Rangers Lt Edward Loustalot, Lt Joseph Randall and Tech Howard Henry who were all killed during the raid, the first three Americans to die on mainland Europe during World War II.

On either side of the beach the two headlands dominate the shoreline. To the east are the sheer chalk cliffs overlooking the harbour where concealed German machine-guns and mortar posts did so much damage to the Essex Scottish. On the top of the hill were the field guns and anti-aircraft batteries that engaged the warships that came close inshore. The western headland, crowned with the old Château, looks down onto White Beach, the landing site of the Royal Hamilton Light Infantry, and provides a panoramic view of the landing beaches. From there it is clear that the headland dominates virtually every square foot of the beachhead and just how vulnerable the Canadians on the beach were.

Carry on over the headland to the west and within less than a mile you descend into Pourville. During the descent pull off the road into the lay-by on the right and you have arrived near the site of the radar station. Below is Green Beach, its wide sweep of shingle totally dominated from this hill. Behind and to the left are the pillboxes and defences that gave so much trouble to Colonel Merritt and his Saskatchewans, although many of these bunkers were built post-1942. Down in the village, just back from the sea, is the bridge over the River Scie, 'Merritt's Bridge', where his supreme valour in the face of the enemy won him the Victoria Cross. From the beach at Pourville if you look to the right towards Dieppe you can see part of the radar station that has collapsed down onto the shore, its foundations on top of the chalk cliff eroded by the endless assault of the sea. In the village by the small church are many memorials to the units who fought at Pourville.

Continuing westwards, on the outskirts of the village of Varengeville at Le Mesnil is the one solitary concrete bunker that remains of 'Hess' Battery, complete with its memorial to 4 Commando. Across the field to the north is the wood in which Sergeant Jimmy Dunning set up his mortar and silenced the coastal guns with a single bomb. Follow the road alongside the wood down to a small car park at the head of the cliffs at Vasterival. From there a path leads down to Orange I Beach. Walk down the near vertical steps to the shore and then turn and look at the towering cliffs behind you and imagine just how Mills-Roberts managed to get his men up that gully on the morning of 19 August 1942. Still further to the west is Orange I Beach at Quiberville where Lord Lovat and his party landed. This is a wide flat beach eminently suitable for landings and one that was consequently defended by concrete pillboxes, which were wiped out by 4 Commando.

Just beyond the headland on the eastern side of Dieppe, overlooking the harbour entrance, is the tiny village of Puys. Blue Beach nestles tightly against the high sea wall just as it did when the Royal Regiment of Canada was immolated against its granite sides. Close by is a memorial to the fallen. Alongside this are the German defences that wrought such carnage. Of all the sites on the battlefield this is the most evocative. This small beach, hemmed in by a high sea wall and overlooked by grassy cliffs studded with concrete pillboxes, became, for a few hours on a hot August morning, a killing ground on a scale that leaves one numb. Standing on the beach looking up at the wall and the looming cliffs, it is perhaps possible to comprehend a little of the horror and despair felt by the young men trapped in this small corner of hell on 19 August 1942.

At Berneval, little remains to be seen except the landing places of the few Commandos who managed to make it ashore. Yellow I Beach is easily accessible, Yellow II Beach less so. The memorial at the top of the gully above Yellow I Beach commemorates the courage of these few men who pressed on with their tasks with resolute determination against such hopeless odds.

The fallen of Operation Jubilee are gathered in the Commonwealth War Cemetery on the southern edge of Dieppe, close to the road to Rouen and Paris. Here Canadians lie alongside Commandos, Royal Marines, seamen and airmen who were killed in the battle.

BIBLIOGRAPHY

Anon, *Raid on Dieppe: Battle Summary No 33*, Naval Staff History (London, 1959)

Anon, *Signal, No 2 October 1942*, Deutscher Verlag (Berlin, 1942)

Atkin, Ronald, *Dieppe 1942: The Disaster*, Macmillan (London, 1980)

Féron, Claude & Bertout, Gérard, *19 Aout 1942 A Dieppe*, Editions Bertout (Luneray, 1992)

Fowler, Will, *The Commandos at Dieppe: Rehearsal for D-Day*, Collins (London, 2002)

Franks, Norman, *The Greatest Air Battle: Dieppe 19th August 1942*, Grubb Street (London, 1992)

Henry, Hugh G., *Dieppe Through The Lens*, Battle of Britain Prints International (London)

Ladd, James, *Commandos and Rangers*, Macdonald & Janes (London, 1978)

Leasor, James, *Green Beach,* Heinemann (London, 1975)

Maguire, Eric, *Dieppe August 19*, Jonathan Cape (London, 1963)

Saunders, Hilary St George, *The Green Beret*, Michael Joseph (London, 1949)

Stacey, Col C. P., *The Canadian Army 1939–1945*, Canadian Ministry of National Defence, (Ottawa, 1948)

INDEX

Figures in **bold** refer to illustrations